JUDY

THE GREATEST CHIMPANZEE THAT EVER LIVED

PREVIOUS WORKS BY RALPH HELFER

The Beauty of The Beasts

Modoc, The Greatest Elephant That Ever Lived

Zamba, The Greatest Lion That Ever Lived

Modoc, The World's Greatest Elephant (Children's Book)

Zamba, The World's Greatest Lion (Children's Book)

Mosey (Children's Book)

The Legend of Modoc, The Lost Years

JUDY
THE GREATEST CHIMPANZEE THAT EVER LIVED

Judy and Ralph

BY RALPH HELFER

Published in the United States.
Published by Legacy.
Books may be purchased for educational, business, or sales promotional use.
www.ralph-helfer.com
info@ralph-helfer.com

First Edition

Book design by Tana Helfer Herbert

Library of Congress Cataloging-in-Publication Data

Helfer, Ralph
JUDY / by
Ralph Helfer. — 1st ed.
p. cm.

ISBN Paperback: 979-8-9912786-3-8
ISBN Hardback: 979-8-9912786-4-5
ISBN eBook: 979-8-9912786-5-2

1. JUDY (Chimpanzee) 2. Animals, Freedom 1. Title
LCCN: 2024925873
Auto Biography and Fiction

Credits for Image, photo insert, and jacket

Tana Helfer Herbert
(Created final Cover Image)
Jacket Design 2024 Tana Helfer Herbert
Cover Digital Image 2024 Tana Helfer Herbert
Cover Photo layover of Judy Courtesy of Ralph Helfer
Layout by Tana Helfer Herbert
Author photograph Courtesy of Ralph Helfer Pg. 3,189 & Bk Cover

DEDICATION

Tana, Cathi, Alicia

With Love

ACKNOWLEDGMENTS

When editors take up the challenge of editing books about subjects they may know little about, they need to be totally committed. The person I chose to edit my book had to be my friend, a person who knew me well enough to understand my idiosyncrasies. My living in Africa, halfway around the world, would also make it most difficult to communicate my thoughts.

I have been most fortunate to have such a great person edit my book. So, with this, I say thank you to Rebecca St. George for her patience and understanding. A talented individual and I treasure her friendship and honesty. Nothing gets by her. As an accomplished writer herself, she was never afraid to speak her mind. Both 'Modoc, The Greatest Elephant That Ever Lived' and 'Zamba, The Greatest Lion That Ever Lived,' would not have been possible without her insight, suggestions, thoughts, and abilities. So, thank you, Rebecca.

To my lovely wife, Toni, who was there in the middle of the night with hot coffee and a cheerful thought to keep me going. Her views and comments pulled me out of a lot of tough spots.

To my daughter, who has always been there for me whether we agreed or did not, she was my personal 'Jiminy Cricket.'

Authors Note

As a writer living in Africa, I find it most difficult to put down my work when storms over Mt. Kenya cause the electricity to go off and the computer shuts down. I race to complete that 'once in a lifetime thought' and the battery goes dead. Often, the elephants knock down the telephone poles, or the locals steal the telephone cables or transformer. And yet I sit on our patio, before dawn, hot coffee in hand, wrapped in a Masai shuka (blanket) and wait for the morning sun to shine its rays upon the snowcapped slopes of Mt. Kenya. It is then that I get my incentive to write. To tell my early life experiences with animals. I watch as the ibis, hornbills, and vultures come to enjoy the foods set out by my wife the night before. There is no fighting for each eats differently.

In my growing up years, King Kong was my idol. Mighty Joe Young followed in his footsteps. As I grew up, the thought of finding giant apes dissipated with the wakening of every dream. Cheetah with his friend, Tarzan, brought primates down to size. It was nice to know that humans could befriend apes. All were smart, strong, bigger than life in many ways, and loyal to those they loved. As a child, they took me in. I knew that whatever was to occur in my life, it would be to befriend the brothers and sisters of my kin.

My thoughts traverse the realm of understanding between humans and apes. Things which we once explored might perhaps need to be reopened to find a better way to communicate between man and animal. Many before us have tried to reach into the core of man/animal understanding. Few have succeeded. In my search for a 'Judy,' I came to find out that apes, like people, were individuals. No two were alike. Also, no two had the same intellect. I reasoned that if there could be a breakthrough in communication, surely it leaves open the possibility that we can open a door into the inner recesses of the narrow intellect of the primitive mind.

This book was meant to be about the life of a chimpanzee who came from the jungles of Africa and her journey to the silver screen. But as I wrote, it came to mind that the true experience was an adventure into the mind of this extraordinary ape, and her ability to live in the human world, to learn its many idiosyncrasies. Judy was able to live in both worlds and be comfortable. She learned from us humans and was able to blend.

In the forty years that I have worked with primates, none has affected me as Judy did. How fortunate I have been to spend a portion of my life with this remarkable animal. She has been my mentor into the world of primates.

It is such a pity that the world cannot find a way to preserve its animals. The future is so dim. I have found myself remembering the era of the dinosaur and thinking of our planet without animals. Some say that the dinosaurs disappeared because of a meteor collision; there was no choice in the matter. Nature had decided their fate. We, on the other hand, do have the power and knowledge to ward off the extinction of animals today. But unfortunately, we have become 'earth gods.' We tell the animals when they shall live or die. Those animals that provide a need for humans will remain the longest. What can a wild animal offer to humans that is so valuable they must give their life for it?

Judy will always live in my heart, not as a primate, but as my friend. She was a true ambassador for all primates.

Chapter 1

The impenetrable jungle woke with the sun yawning its way over the Congo's Verunga Mountains. Gray mist in the valley below dissolved as the sun's burning rays pierced its veil.

The bark of a creature was heard breaking the stillness. Another bark. This one was different. More shrill, more foreboding. The mist separated to reveal the face of a hairy ape, its eyes wide and startling. It peered through the thin veneer and then was gone.

An old 1930s, four-cylinder Ford pickup truck bounced over the rough terrain.

"Where the bloody hell did you get this piece of junk? The damn thing will fall apart before we find any apes."

Jac, a 60ish, potbellied, balding, boorish man, stood in the back of the pickup holding onto a length of leather tied to the hooks welded to the side of the truck. Without the leather, he would surely have lost his balance. The ancient jalopy crashed its way through the thick tangle of tropical vines and growth. At each jolt, Jac crunched his burned-out cigar between a set of broken yellow teeth. Spittle ran down his chin.

This was a 'spiritual' jungle, at least that's what the locals called it. They believed that their God lived there and kept it filled with wildlife; flocks of multicolored birds, trees centuries old. Unnamed rivers raced down the mountain, gullies overflowed, cascading through the narrows solid with the broken igneous rock of a million years past. Nearby, a raging river formed islands of sand banks; old fallen trees clogged the waterways rushing downstream tempering its power, breaking it into streams, then rivulets, and finally vessels of small potholes thick with the muck from the mountain above. These kept the Ford slipping and sliding.

Jac kept his trained poacher's eyes on the branches above. The thickness of the canopy prevented the rays of the sun from penetrating to the jungle floor. From its humid wetness drifted a sweet overpowering pungent musk.

"We've been here all morning, ain't seen a thing," fumed Jac.

Under the canopy back in the darkness - a movement.

"Not true, my man," said Churney, keeping one hand on the steering wheel while supporting a pair of horn-rimmed eyeglasses from falling off his face. He was a small man and sharp of wit, but useless when it came to any kind of adversity. He sported a cap that said, "Be Brave" on it. The little man pointed to a huge fig tree that seemed to touch the sky. Close to the top, nestled under the canopy in an elbow of thick branches, there appeared to be a black moving thing.

"Look there," he said and pointed, leaning out the window.

"What? Where? Ahh! There's nothing there. Shit."

"Not that tree, this one." Again, Churney pointed an exaggerated wiggling finger at a tree.

Near the top, squeezed into the thicket of sturdy branches, sat a large female chimpanzee. Close to her, a young one straddled her back, small arms clutching her neck. The young chimp could clearly feel his mother tense up. He took a tighter grip on her and buried his head into her shoulder.

Both were petrified of the intruders below. She looked to an adjoining tree in hopes she could jump to it, but with the young one on her back, she realized it was not close enough. She could only wait until they left.

"Pull up, pull up!" yelled Jac.

Churney jammed his foot on the brake; the car lurched against a thicket of bush. Jac stumbled out of the car and peered up the tree at the chimps huddled at the top.

"Get me my 30-odd-6. That should reach them."

Churney scrambled and pulled out an old rifle no longer manufactured. He grabbed a handful of shells and, nearly falling out of the vehicle, handed them to Jac. He loaded the gun with a few shells and cocked the rifle to put a shell in the chamber.

"This should do it," he said, murmuring to himself. "Doesn't make a big hole so the pelt will be usable."

He found a good spot to settle down and rested the stock of the gun against a tree stump. Lying spread out on the ground, he took aim at the chimp.

"Which one first?" asked Churney.

"Stupid! The big one, of course. If I go for the little guy and miss, the mother might take him further into the brush. Might not get a second chance. Besides, the little guy is riding piggyback so I can't get a clear shot anyhow."

"What if you hit the young one by accident?"

"What if? The locals will buy any bush meat or skin. They don't care. And their favorite, after gorilla, is chimp. That youngster up there will bring a lot of shekels dead or alive." Jac threw his dilapidated stogy on the ground and wiped the brown spittle from his jaw with the back of his hand.

"The old mommy is hiding behind the branch," he whispered, as though the chimps could hear him. Then, arching the rifle directly at the chimps, he waited. As things grew quiet, the mama chimp, as if getting impatient, leaned forward to see if the strange creatures had gone.

That was all Jac needed. The thunderous shot vibrated throughout the jungle for miles around. Flocks of birds flew in a panic, scared by what they heard rather than what they saw. The gathering elephants at the river bolted in all directions, trumpeting, not knowing which way to go. The bullet passed through the mother's temple, clean.

She sat for a moment and then, as though in slow motion, with eyes open, the young chimp still clutching her, she fell. Slow at first - then faster. The young chimp held on, waiting for his mother to grab a branch as she always did, swinging from one to another, traveling through the trees. She fell, hitting branches on the way down slowing her fall. The young chimp, hit by twigs, leaves, and bumped by branches, hung on. She hit hard, dislodging the young chimp from her back. He rolled away. Numb.

A perfect shot.

"God damn, I'm good!" he yelled, as he watched the chimps fall. "Quick, grab the young one before it gets away."

Both men scrambled for the young chimp that stumbled, bewildered, through the brush confused, disoriented. He felt hands grab him as they threw him into a dark metal box. Peeking through a crack at the edge of the box, he saw the men drag his mother into the truck. Why didn't she move, run away? he thought. He sat in the corner licking a trickle of blood that oozed from his arm as they drove the rough road back to the poachers' place.

Churney pulled the truck up to a dilapidated barn. While he opened the big wooden framed barn doors, Jac reached in the box and grabbed the chimp. The chimp screamed and tried to bite him, but Jac was too strong for him.

He was yanked out of the box, carried into the barn, and thrown into a room full of junk auto parts. The room was completely sealed off with steel wire mesh. The chimp limped over to an old car body frame and hid behind it. Finding a ragged, oil-stained blanket, he wrapped it around himself, leaving a portion to put over his head. His body was still sore from the fall, with cuts from the twigs. He shivered, not from cold, but from fear.

Fear of the unknown.

He wanted his mother to cuddle him; assure him that all was well. He noticed across the way two or three cages similar to his. There were four or five chimps and a smattering of small monkeys imprisoned in them.

He was not alone. From out of the junk in the back of the enclosure came another chimp-like animal. Twice his size with sparse long red hair, it ambled over to the chimp and sat in front of him. The chimp, still shivering, looked at this strange ape. He offered a low 'ohhh' sound. The red-haired ape answered back but in a different tone of voice. He extended the back of his hand to the chimp, who smelled his friendliness. Then the stranger reached over and pulled the young chimp to him. They embraced and a sense of warmth coursed through the little chimp. It reminded him of the way his mother had held him. The two hugged each other and, with the dirty oil sack, they covered themselves as sleep overcame them both. The chimp felt if he couldn't see the bad humans they couldn't see him.

In the weeks that followed, the two became inseparable. One didn't move without the other. The chimp rarely let go of the orang's hand. If he did it was to let him grab hold of some of the long red hair. Occasionally, he would jump to the orang's back and be carried around like his mama use to do. But he was too heavy and the ride didn't last long. They were thrown a meager amount of food once a day. This they shared quietly, calmly. As the days passed, they learned several tricks about how to live with the strangers - one was not to hang on the cage's mesh wire when the small man came into the barn. Their fingers would be whipped with his walking stick or anything else that was handy. They learned to drink all the water that was brought to them because it would be taken away within minutes.

"Don't want the place to become a sloppy muddy mess when customers come," the small man barked.

The two men ran a lucrative poaching business in the heart of the jungle just outside of the town of Goma, in the Congo of Uganda. This area was famous for troupes of gorillas that frequented the surrounding jungle. The poachers knew that many tourists came to see them. Although there were many chimps in the area, it was really the gorillas that brought the tourists.

So the poachers had to be careful. Some of the visitors were fanatical animal lovers and when they heard that animal parts, especially gorilla, were being sold as trinkets, they would act violently - in some cases instigating riots, throwing rocks and causing disturbances.

The local police did little to nothing to stop the poachers as most received a substantial amount each time a sale was made. The primates were butchered and their meat called "bush meat" was sold locally to the wealthy at a price the poor could not afford. A local man who called himself a taxidermist, would skin any animal brought to him. The bodies were denuded, the skin stretched out and salt rubbed into the back side of it. After a while the skin would harden. To soften, it was buffed over a makeshift wooden roller till all the fiber was broken down. The heads of the animals were skinned same as the body. The head bones were soaked in hot water just long enough for the meat to loosen and be removed. Then it was dipped into special liquid for a night. When retrieved in the morning the skull bones had become hard as rock. The skin, when ready, was stretched over the skull and brushed out awaiting the return of the buyer for pickup. Usually the heads, hand and feet went to the Middle Eastern countries up north saving a few for the local tourists. They would send their 'associates' to buy the items as they didn't want any publicity that could hurt their image. If you were to visit some of the wealthy homes in certain countries, you would most likely see the head of a primate proudly featured on their fireplace mantel. The most expensive was a gorilla head. It was not unusual to pay $50,000 for a good head. For a chimp, they paid $10,000.

Primate hands were treated and cupped to form ashtrays with fingers extended and curled upright to hold cigarettes. Some of the more ignorant tourists had no idea of the rarity of these animals. They simply wanted to have one of these 'trinkets' to take back home to show off to their friends. Little did they know that once the custom officers at the airport found them in their luggage, they would be arrested, miss their flight, and made to pay a handsome fine.

These custom officials were tipped off by the poachers as to who had purchased the pieces so they knew exactly which luggage to open. Once the heads and other animal paraphernalia were confiscated, the officers would sell them back to the poachers and the routine was perpetuated again. This way the police profited by the front and back of the sale. If, on the other hand, the client was a well-to-do individual, then the officers were told to let him pass and the poachers would give them their cut without the arresting procedure.

The two simian friends were never idle. Their favorite time was spent preening each other. They would spend hours at a time parting each other's hair scraping with their nails at any loose dry skin particles, perhaps a small bug who hitched a ride rather than stay in the junk yard. Scabbed were picked, noses as well were included in their 'jungle' salon.

They were terrified whenever the men came close to their cage. The chimp remembered what they had done to his mother. The fall from the tree, the dragging of her lifeless body away. Instinctively they knew they had to get away.

They had checked out every inch of their prison and found one small opening in the back of the compound underneath a pile of old car parts. They worked on it every chance they got - digging, pulling, biting, until their gums and hands bled.

One early morning, the big barn door opened and in walked Jac. With him were two strangers. One, an Arab dressed in an expensive silk white tiraz, the other a touristy-looking man sporting a tailored safari outfit.

He was well known to the poachers and always brought prospective buyers, as was the case in point. The Arab was a wealthy oil broker who had a passion for gathering a collection of heads - including human. The hard-to-find headhunter tribes from the South American jungles had supplied him with a few. It was told that many victims were killed just to keep the man in supply.

"This way, gentlemen," spoke Jac, as he guided them over to the 'junk yard' cage. The two apes sat at the far end on one of the beat-up engines on top of the oil soaked rag. They stared back at the strangers, showing no emotion, only a placid look of hidden disdain. They had become used to Jac bringing in people. Their fear would be if he decided to come inside the cage.

"What in the world? Where did you get an orangutan?" asked the safari man. "They're not from Africa at all."

"I got him from the zoo. They didn't want to sell him but everything has a price, right?" He smiled.

"I figured he would bring a good price on the market".

"They're quite rare, you know," said the Arab.

"Yeah, but no more than a gorilla."

"Aren't you afraid of being caught?" asked the Arab, eyeing the orang.

"By whom? The local cops? Ha! No way. They make too much out of our deals."

"How much are you asking?"

"Well, for his head $8,000.00. The meat I can sell locally."

He thought for a moment. "When he is ready contact me; I will be most interested."

"And the chimp?" asked Jac.

"He is a bit small but... o.k., prepare him. I will have my people pick him up along with the orang next month."

Having said his piece, the Arab turned and, without a goodbye, let alone a handshake, left.

Jac was elated. This fellow never even mentioned the cost. That was always a sign of wealth. He knew he would get a good sum of money for the orang.

Jac sat contemplating on how he was going to spend the money.

However, the two primates had other plans. True, they had no idea what was in store for them but their timing was right and instinctively they knew they had to get away. They had managed to twist some of the wire mesh fence around their cage until it broke. They squeezed out around midnight and took off into the jungle - free.

Early morning. A loud scream came from the barn. It was Jac. He had gone to check on his animals only to find them gone. When the poachers discovered they had escaped, he was furious. Yelling for Churney, he set out to find them. They hunted night and day but to no avail.

For the next two days and nights the apes ran. Grabbing a banana here, a mango fruit there, they never stopped. Their bodies were hurting, their feet sore and bloody from the jungle floor. Being arboreal animals, their feet weren't adapted to running on the ground - and surely for not such an extended run as this.

The two apes hid themselves well and by the second week were miles away from the poachers' camp.

As time passed, they found themselves on the outskirts of a farming community at the edge of the jungle.

They saw humans working in fields of food. All kinds of food. Being vegetarians, they were delighted to find such a wonderful food supply and felt that this would be a good place to stay. They picked a tall, heavily foliaged fig tree near to the farm and built themselves a nest at the top. Most primates lived in the trees, keeping away from the dangerous animals that frequented the ground below. Chimps made a great meal for most predators, especially leopards and they climb trees. But it was the best they could do.

The nest was made of whatever they could pluck from the trees, like branches, twigs, and leaves to keep them warm, safe, and secure.

At night while the humans slept, they would sneak down into the farms and raid the food they most enjoyed. Although primates didn't usually travel on the ground at night due to the dangers, this was a different matter. It was about survival. The food was plentiful here and with so many humans around during the daylight hours, they had no choice. The young chimp depended a lot on his larger red-haired friend. He looked up to him to guide them down the right paths, locate different food, and steer them away from the humans.

It was during a very early morning return from the fields to their tree nest that a danger awaited them. The moon, having moved on for the month, left the jungle quite dark. They climbed the tree, each carrying what they could from the farm.

As they approached their nest, the orang sensed something was wrong. The nest was in shambles and destroyed. Most of the twigs and branches hung over the edge, ready to fall to the ground below.

There was a movement back in the shadows behind where the nest used to be. The apes dropped their food supply and backed up, frightened yet curious as to what it was.

Then they saw it - a huge python coiled inside the darkness waiting!

The chimp made a near silent whimper and in so doing, slipped on the branch he was standing on. A few leaves fell. A twig creaked. The snake, alerted to the noise, slithered out into the open looking for what had caused the disturbance. He was enormous - thick as the main branch of the tree and as long as the vine that touched the ground.

Then it saw them.

With head held high, it came at them. Arched in a strike position, it struck mouth open, coils curled ready to engulf whatever prey they found. A near miss! The apes screamed and ran - each climbing in a different direction. They jumped to another tree and another tree after that. The snake, confused for a moment, lost precious time as the apes raced away. Then suddenly, the snake was in hot pursuit, but that moment of hesitation cost the snake his meal.

Up and away, they went far from the jaws of the giant reptile. They met up, both hitting the ground at the same time, running so fast that they didn't stop for an hour - until the chimp ran out of breath.

The snake was not to be seen. No way were they going back to the tree nest. Instead, they continued their direction away from the place where they were almost killed.

A week later found them situated in another tree. It was tall and scant of leaves, except at the top. This is where they built a shabby nest. From the ground up, they ripped out every branch, leaf, and twig that obstructed their outlook from their nest. Without the leaves and branches blocking their view, they could see forever. Even a month later, both sometimes still woke in the middle of the night screaming - maybe because a branch moved from the wind or one of them had a bad dream.

Their new area allowed the farmlands to come right up to the jungle's edge. A bit too close. They could hear the farmers picking their crops and, in some cases, see them working in the fields. But they were content. Their tree offered good security plus an abundance of food.

They raided the farms every third night. They could only take so much food back with them. Sometimes, rather than bring some food back, they sat and ate. A few times, they fell asleep in the tomato patch or wherever they happened to be. They felt quite secure as the farmers left early and the farm was devoid of humans - or so they thought.

One night their luck ran out. It happened quickly. A sliver of the moon cast a pale gloom over the farm. Not enough to see by but enough for a group of men armed with nets, pitchforks, baseball bats, and flashlights to converge on the sleeping pair. Bright lights shone in a circle around them. Voices rang out.

"Kill the bastards!"

"Throw the damn net. Here! Here!"

A few bats hit their mark as well as the stabbing of pitchforks.

"I think I got one!"

Then flashing lights; shadows of both men and beasts scrambling around made it impossible to tell who was who. The apes were terrified and tried to bite their way through the net but to no avail.

The men from the local farms had seen the damage to their crops, and decided to band together and rid the area of the culprits.

Voices echoed in the dark.

"What now?" asked one of the farmhands. "It's too dark to see what's in the net. They're some kind of apes."

"What should we do with them?"

"Let's take them up to Steve's place. He'll know."

The men slid long strong poles through the netting and with a few on either side, lifted them to their shoulders, and carried the frightened apes toward a local farmhouse. Steve Mathers, the owner of the farm and Karimi, his head man met them on arrival.

"We got the animals that have been raiding our crops. You should have been there."

"What are they?"

"I don't know. Apes of some kind."

They carried the net and the intruders into the farm equipment room.

"Flip on the lights," yelled someone in the dark.

Bright lights blasted the room into a blinding whiteness. The room was a rather large place that housed all the crop seed, bags of fertilizer, hand tools, hoses, and a miscellaneous array of other items. In the center of the room was a large table used to sort plants.

"Put them up on the table so we can have a look at them."

Whatever was on the table was quickly swiped to the floor. The men stood around glaring at the animals. Both apes were holding each other, shaking and petrified. Blood oozed from multiple wounds. They looked out through the heavy netting to a group of human creatures, the same ones they had seen in the fields. They stank from their strong sweat which told the apes they were a dangerous hostile enemy. If a man got too close to the net the apes lashed out, whopping the net with their fists. Other times biting the thick weave.

"Now what do we do?" asked one of the farmhands to no one in particular.

"Well, we can either dispose of them now, sell their bodies to the locals or . . ."

". . . or we could take them alive to the poachers. They would give a better price for them."

The men looked tired from the capture and wanted to get it over with.

"Yes or no? Which will it be?"

"Kill them now. We don't have the time to drive them all the way to the poachers' place."

"Yeah, o.k. Who wants to do it?"

"We'll all do it. Better that way."

"How?"

"How what?"

"How do we do it?"

"Well, just beat them."

"Ugh! That's brutal."

"Then use the pitchfork."

"Nah, too messy."

"Look, we're farmers. We butcher cows, sheep, and goats all the time," said one grizzly old timer.

"Yeah, but these are, well, more human."

Both the apes were looking up at the farmers. Huddled together, they were indeed a sorry sight.

"Well then," he said, "the money's better if we deliver them alive. The poachers' place isn't that far. I'll take them in the morning."

"Yeah, let those guys do the dirty work," spoke up one of the men.

"Steve. What do you think?" asked another.

Steve had been looking at the apes and was not participating in the discussion. He seemed distant and absorbed in what he was thinking. Finally, he addressed the men.

"Ya know, if it wasn't so late I'd get Doc Berk up here to treat them."

A surprised murmur swept over the group.

"What?" said Karimi in disbelief. "I don't mean to be disrespectful, Mr. Steve, but why?"

"They're in pain, Karimi, and no animal should be allowed to suffer."

Karimi, an African of the Buganda tribe, had been with Steve for over ten years. A stocky, barrel-chested black man of average height, they had met when Steve was still going to the university. Steve needed to do a paper on farming among the primitive people. He wanted to demonstrate that due to hardship, they had never had a chance to advance. Yet, through their struggles, they had developed a method of cultivating crops that was far more productive than the more modern machinery. Steve hired him to supervise his staff and learn the technique. He stayed on and ended up running the farm under Steve's tutelage.

"First thing in the morning you get Doc on the phone and have him come. We'll keep them here tonight. I'll decide what to do with them after Doc treats them. Maybe there won't be a need to decide seeing the way they look."

"Where do you want to put them for the night?"

"Just leave them where they are. It stays warm in here so they'll be as good as can be expected where they are."

"That net is pretty strong so I guess it will hold them," said Karimi.

Steve and the men exited the room shutting off the lights as they left. The two apes sat quietly holding each other in the dark. Occasionally one whimpered from the pain caused by the bats and pitchforks.

A minute later, the door opened. Steve peered into the dark room. He was torn between telling his wife or waiting till morning. Best not to tell. There was nothing that could be done till morning and she would worry all night about them. He hesitated for a moment then closed the door.

Chapter 2

The rays of the morning sunlight shone through the window resting on the two apes sitting in the net holding each other. They were awake early. Neither had slept much, if at all, what with the pain from their injuries.

The bleeding had stopped, the blood having coagulated on their skin and hair. Both were feeling the pain throughout their bodies. They felt stiff and nauseated. Both had defecated and urinated causing the room to reek of the foul odor. The chimp sat, slowly pulling out bits of dirt, grass, dried blood, and scabs from the orang who was too much in pain to care for himself. The door opened and Steve and his headman, Karimi, entered.

"Whew! That's rank," said Karimi, waving both his hands in front of his face.

"Yeah," said Steve. "Wow, go get some help so we can get them out of here."

The apes, petrified of the men and not knowing what they might do, squeezed themselves as far back in the net as they could, holding each other, trying to hide.

While waiting for the help to arrive, Steve went over and sat close to them. The chimp made some loud 'oho oho' sounds, more out of fear than aggression. The orang did nothing. His eyes were half-closed and he looked the worst of the two. Steve saw the suffering they were experiencing but there was nothing he could do till the vet arrived. A couple of Steve's men came in.

"Here's the guys, Boss," said Karimi.

"Wow! That smarts," said one of them, putting his handkerchief to his nose.

"What's up, Boss?" the other fellow said trying not to notice the smell in the room.

Steve motioned to the poles used to carry the apes last night. "Grab those poles. Let's get these apes out of here and into some fresh air."

The two men, along with Karimi and Steve, slid the poles through the netting, hefted the two animals up and out the door, setting them down on a patch of grass in front of the building.

"A couple of you guys go and clean out the room the apes were in," said Karimi, adding with a smile, "It's a tough job but someone has to do it."

Steve couldn't take his eyes off the apes. "Ya know, I think I'll keep them."

"What?" said Karimi. "Are you crazy or something?" He knew he was out of line to say that to his boss but he had worked for him for many years and to keep them just didn't make any sense to him. "Sorry, Boss, but ... I mean, why? They eat a lot, need care and looking after their wounds. If they live, they'll need of a vet for some time."

"So?"

"So why keep them?

Steve thought awhile. "You know, Karimi, I have always been against this poacher thing. They're butchers!" he exclaimed. "They cut up and sell primate meat to the locals. Why, it's like eating human flesh. These apes are endangered, for Christ's sakes. There's only a few of them left. Why would I want to see them hanging from the butchers' hooks?"

Then, as an afterthought, he said, "And the worst is in the marketplace. People actually buy ape-hand ashtrays. And worst of all, even the police are in on it. They make so much money. They even know where the poachers live and do nothing."

"Yeah, they have been seen at their place." added Karimi.

"Probably getting their cut of a recent sale."

"Well, it's true. Every time I think of those bastards, I get angry too," said Karimi. "But we have to think of our crops. Last year was a bad season; the drought was forever. We never had a drought in this part of the country before."

"It's because of this global warming thing," voiced Steve.

"I know, that's my point. What happens if we have another drought? If the animals of the forest keep eating our produce and the drought hits, well, you know where I'm going with this."

"Yeah, but I just don't want to contribute to what they are doing."

Karimi thought for a moment. "You're right. Look, if they get well, why not just turn them loose, just not around the farm."

"That's what I intend on doing, but first we've got to treat their wounds."

"They might just die from their injuries."

"Well whatever. Did you call the vet?"

"Sure did. He's on the way."

"Last night we were ready to do them in. Maybe it would have been better than letting them suffer," said Karimi.

"Not if they make it," Steve commented solemnly.

It was early morning before Dr. Berk, the vet, arrived. Tall, lean, and wearing thick spectacles, he was more like a country doctor than a bush vet. He drove a small-sized Land Rover with a red cross on both sides.

After a few handshakes.

"You sure got here quick," said Steve.

"Whoever called said it was an emergency."

Steve looked at Karimi with a smile.

Coming across the yard was Marti, Steve's wife. She, like Karimi, was of the Buganda tribe. They were an influential upper-class people respected by other tribes for their stand on helping those who were destitute as well as supporting the women's rights movement. A beauty in her own right, her strong dark features were as an ancient carved princess. Brought up in an English school, her speech was flawless and coupled with quite a British accent. She had high cheekbones, full lips, and a straight nose. She was a proud person who was able to handle the most difficult situations.

"What in the world…!" she exclaimed.

She crouched down to see the two apes. "Good Lord, what a mess. Steve, what happened?"

"Our neighbors found them raiding their crops last night and well, almost did them in."

"Why didn't you let me know?"

"There was nothing anyone could have done," he explained. "Even though they're in pain, they're still wild animals and could give quite a bite if we tried to handle them. And besides, what could we do?:

"Hi, Marti," said the doctor. They knew each other from the times he had come to the farm to treat their livestock.

"Hi, Doc. Let me know if you need any help."

"Sure will," he said.

"Doc just arrived so let's see if we can get them back in shape," said Steve.

Dr. Berk got his medicine bag, a rather long, large bag out of the back of the Rover and they headed towards where the apes were being held on the lawn. He noticed Steve looking at the bag. He answered before asked. "You never know what you may run into. So, I take it all."

"The whole hospital?"

"Just about," he replied with a smile.

"Why the red cross out on your Rover, Doc?"

"There are so few doctors out here, I sub-in whenever necessary."

"You mean treating humans?"

"Yeah. Better than doing nothing."

"Hmmm," said Steve.

Dr. Berk went over to the apes and kneeling down, studied them for a while.

The chimp, startled by his action let out a yelp and smacked the net with the back of his hand.

"They look in bad shape. Want me to put them down?" he asked, shaking his head at the condition they were in.

"No. See what you can do for them first."

Steve seemed determined to try to save them.

The vet took a thin long box out of his bag and opened it. Lying in a padded velvet lining were two guns, one a rifle, the other a pistol.

Steve was alarmed. "Wait a sec, Doc . . ."

"Don't worry. These are tranquilizer guns. It's the only way to anesthetize them."

When the chimp saw the rifle, he went berserk. He remembered seeing Jac's gun before he and his mother came crashing to the earth. He screamed at the top of his lungs, chewed at the rope, and did summersaults while spraying a loose stool everywhere.

"Look at that reaction. You'd think he knew what a gun was," said Karimi.

"We won't need the rifle. It's too close to use it. The pistol will do just fine," offered Doc. As soon as he put the rifle away, the chimp stopped screaming.

"Are they safe?"

"It all depends. Operating is not easy."

Doc opened up the gun case to show Steve how the gun worked. There were three extremely important things to be aware of. First, you had to be accurate. If you missed the spot that the dart must hit and instead hit a bone, it could shatter it causing a completely new injury, or worse, you could hit an organ and that could cause instant death.

Second, seeing as the amount of drug used was based on the weight of the animal and you weren't in a position to weigh the animal, you had to guess its weight. Over or under by a large margin would either not put the animal down or overdose it and it would never awaken.

The third and final thing you had to do was gauge the strength of the dart. If it was too powerful, it could act as a bullet and go clear through the animal or if it were not strong enough, it would just bounce off the skin.

"Not as easy as it looks," said Steve.

Doc Berk unscrewed the feathered end of the dart and carefully dripped in a small amount of the serum.

Once done he screwed on the back and inserted the dart into the gun.

"I'll start with the orangutan. He's the one with the most serious injury."

Homing in on the animal's hind leg, the only area that had some muscle, he took careful aim and pulled the trigger.

The pistol made a pop sound as the orang felt the dart hit his body. His reaction was to grab the dart and pull it out biting the bright colored feathers at the end. There wasn't any pain, only the shock of the needle penetrating his leg.

It was but a few minutes after the dart hit home that the orang toppled over and lapsed into a deep sleep. The chimp ran over to him uttering his 'oho oho,' as he had seen his mother do the same thing and the bad men had dragged her away never to see him again. He panicked, which drove him into a frenzy. He screamed, beat his chest, his eyes glowed red at the vet. Doc had difficulty getting a bead on the chimp's leg muscle. He wasn't still a minute. He had used far less serum due to his smaller size. The pop of the gun was heard and shortly thereafter the chimp succumbed.

"The room is ready, Mr. Steve sir," said one of the staff.

"Take them inside," said Steve. "It's the best place for the doctor to work on them."

The men untied the heavy rope and reaching in carried the two apes into the room. Laying them side by side on the table.

They had done a good job cleaning the room, even to the point of spraying a cleansing liquid that smelled like perfume. The same big table that the apes had been brought to the night before was cleaned and ready for whatever had to be done.

Doc gave them a quick once over.

"I'll start with the orang. His injuries are more serious."

Then he said, "Well, it's a male about four years old. The chimp is younger, maybe three. And it's a female."

He opened his medical bag and proceeded to take out the items he needed. These he lay on a clean white cloth. Sutures, scalpels, and needles were dropped in a shallow pan of alcohol. All needed to be kept sterile.

"Marti, I can use your help."

"Sure, Doc," answered Marti.

Doc knew that Marti had been a medical student at the university, as she had helped him in the past with the livestock. She automatically took over the role of the doctor's assistant.

Dr. Berk went to work doing all he could to save them. He cleaned the wounds, cutting where necessary, injecting antibiotics, and suturing. For the better part of an hour, Doc Berk worked to save the apes. Injections were given to prevent bleeding. Hair was shaved around each wound. The holes and injuries cleaned out, shreds of skin and meat cut away, powerful antiseptics poured into the open wounds, sutures sewed the big wounds closed. Shots of penicillin and streptomycin were given.

"How they doing, Doc?" Steve finally asked.

"Well, the orang is the worst," he said. "He has two deep punctures - one in the thigh, another in the arm and side. His head has a swollen area as big as an egg. Then a few other minor cuts and bruises."

"I think he was trying to protect the chimp," said one of the farmhands.

"Yeah, well you guys sure went to work on them," said Doc.

Bula, a mild-mannered farmer, who ran a small farm nearby, had volunteered to help out, but was hurting over the whole thing. You could see he felt guilty about what happened. He spoke to the doctor as he prepared his instruments.

"I really feel sorry for them, Doc," he said earnestly. "We didn't know what was in the net. It was dark and … and well, with all the men scrambling in the dark, it just got out of hand. We know now it shouldn't have happened. Hope you can save them. I really feel bad."

Mateebi, one of the hard-hearted ones spoke up. He seemed to have had enough of Bula's gibbering.

"So go to church already. Look, it happened. They were eating our food. Food that our wives and children need, so what we did wasn't wrong."

Both men stopped what they were doing and approached each other. Both were red faced.

"Yes, it was! We didn't have to be so tough on them. We could have…"

Steve stepped into what was getting out of hand.

"Hey! Hey! Not here, not now. It was my decision to do what we can to save these little guys. If you want to beef about whether it was right or wrong, take it up with me, not each other. Doc here can patch up the loser."

Everybody had a good laugh and things quieted down. Doc was half-listening to their 'confessions.'

"Let's just see if we can right the wrong, o.k.?" he murmured as he worked. "Looks like the chimp got off lucky. Her injuries are minor in comparison. One puncture here," he said, pointing to her leg, "and another on the shoulder."

"Will they make it?" Steve asked, watching the vet work with intensity.

"The bigger guy, well, I'm not sure. But the other one is tough and her injuries aren't as bad. Should be o.k. Both will need a lot of care. I'll leave some medication for Marti to administer."

"Uh, how are we going to handle that?"

"I'll leave Marti with some oral drugs to combat the infection. Just mix it in their water," he said. "If later you get a chance, put some of this penicillin powder on their wounds."

"Fat chance," said Karimi.

"Well, maybe when they get well they'll be more trusting."

Then speaking to Marti, Doc said, "It's important that you follow the direction explicitly. The problem is, they've both lost a lot of blood, and I don't have any plasma for animals."

"Hey, Mateebi, why don't you give some? You look just like them," said Bula, still pressing his button.

"Ha ha. Funny man," replied Mateebi, handling the jab.

Once done, the apes were taken out and laid on the green lawn. The day was quite warm and the grass seemed to be the best place for them until a cage or something was found to keep them in.

"Where are you going to put them when they wake up? They're going to be a handful," said the doctor.

"How long until they come up?" asked Steve.

"Hmm, perhaps an hour, maybe a bit more. Being weak, their systems will react a lot slower."

"We'll find a place."

Steve paid the good doctor his wages, handed him a quick beer, all gave their thanks, and after a round of handshakes, the doctor was on his way.

"Nice guy," said Steve. "Wouldn't mind him working on me if the time ever comes. Now then, where to put them?"

Everybody had fanned out to find a place to put the two still sleeping patients but reported back without any luck.

"Can't find a place that would work."

"I haven't a clue where to put them."

Marti thought for a moment. "Why not use one of the stalls in the old tractor barn? It won't take much fixing up and it's all enclosed."

"Good idea," Steve said. "Hey, guys!" he called. "Found a place. Let's go."

"Steve . . .?" she yelled after him. "Why don't I clean up the apes while you get the tractor barn ready? They're covered in blood and poop."

"O.k. but be gentle. Those injuries must be quite painful. We don't want to open up any stiches. If they start to wake up, call me."

"Don't worry; the way they look, I'm sure they will be out for quite a while."

She prepared a warm bath for the two apes in a large tub of warm water. She got old towels from the garage and bathing soap from the house. Then, with the assistance from some of the men, one by one, the apes were gently lowered into the shallow water, careful not to let any water get in their noses. She gently soaped and washed their bodies. Steve would have laughed if he saw her pour perfume into the bath water. A brisk towel drying followed. Steve returned to see how she was doing.

"They're still sleeping like babies," was Marti's smiling remark. But suddenly she couldn't hold in her feelings any longer. "Steve, how could the men have been so brutal?"

"The men weren't our workers. They were from the surrounding farms. They took it on themselves to rid the area of any animal that might take food out of their mouths. You know, with the weather changes going on, the crops have taken a beating. These people aren't into the animals as we are. They think survival. They're primitive farm laborers who have been here long before we came. Their small farms are all they have to exist on. These are people who have lived in these jungles for most, if not all, of their lives and are the same people who would buy ape meat in town. Animals to them are here to eat or work - nothing more."

Marti knew what Steve was saying. She just hated to hear that her neighboring friends, the Blacks of the Congo, would do such a thing.

"Well, I hope these guys make it. They're really adorable."

"'Til they get older."

"Then what?"

"They will learn our ways and if not trained properly, become very spoiled and . . ." he hesitated.

"And what?" she asked.

"Dangerous."

"It's hard to believe looking at them now."

"Just like humans. Right?"

"Yeah. Just like us."

Karimi walked over with some of the men. "Barn's ready, Boss. I think it will hold them."

Marti saw to it that an abundance of vegetables from the plantation as well as fruit from the jungle was set in the barn that included plantains, bananas, mangos, apples, carrots, and tomatoes. She had put plenty of water in the barn. A separate bowl of warm milk was also put in. For bedding, they had arranged a large bin that the cattle had used as a feeding trough. It was filled with soft grass and plenty of cloth bags used during the packing season to haul the food to the big market in Goma.

Steve knew that primates slept in trees but not having the time to build something high off the ground, he figured this would do for the present, plus being low to the ground would allow him and his hands to be close to the apes and able to better care for them. Being up high would only make it more difficult.

The apes were just waking up when they were carried into their new home. It wasn't until six in the evening that they started to sit up and look around. Slowly the chimp woke first, sleepy-eyed, unsteady, followed by the orang. When the chimp saw her buddy the orang she nearly fell down running to get to him. Once there, she saw that her buddy was alive and although wobbly was trying to stand. She made her chimp 'oh! oh!' sounds of affection and couldn't keep her hands off him. An hour passed before they noticed the food and drink. Neither ate much but the milk and half the water was downed quickly.

Steve and his men had done a temporary but good job converting the old tractor stalls into the apes' new home. Strong nine-gauge farm wire was stretched around it. Heavy timber for the roof and a heavy oak door finished off a job well done.

It was touch and go for the next few days. Marti slept in the barn next to the stall for the first couple of nights. It was her way. She had always been a compassionate person. She had never had children of her own and her need to care was always foremost in her thoughts.

She saw to it that she administered the medicine on time. They didn't eat much and the orang slept most of the time. There were times when Marti would wake early in the morning and look through the cage fence to see if they were o.k. Only until they stirred did she know if they were still alive or not.

As time went by, the primates began to relax. They walked around, exploring each corner just as they had done in the last cage they were in. This time they did not check for an opening to escape. Whether too sick and feeble, they were content to stay where they were. The chimp did her best to care for her orang friend. She cuddled him keeping him warm especially when he shivered. She preened him often and constantly licked the wounds as the scabs flaked off to be sure they were kept clean. They accepted hand feeding from the woman and by the end of the first week the orang allowed Marti to reach in and put medicine on his wounds. He would lick it off thinking it was food until the bad taste got to him and he would leave it on. The chimp accepted her brushing her back with a long handle brush. Only the men were not allowed to approach. If they did, it triggered an outburst of hostility.

That night after dinner, Marti and Steve were sitting around the fire in the living room. The subject came up about selling them.

"No way, Steve. They're just getting to trust us. You want those murderers to hack them up?" Marti was adamant.

"I wouldn't sell them to those guys. I was thinking of a zoo or perhaps turning them loose."

"And risk those idiots finding them. No way. They're here to stay."

Steve knew that when his wife made up her mind there wasn't much chance of changing it. After a moment's pause he said, "Well, they should have names then. What are you going to call them?"

"My, I never gave that any thought."

"You can't just keep calling them 'hey' or 'you.' How about calling the chimp, Marti?"

"That's my name!" Marti exclaimed.

"I know." Steve smiled. "But she seems as independent and determined as you. Both traits that I love. And she's feisty."

"Thanks a lot," said Marti, with a tongue in cheek look. "O.k., it would be an honor to be named after such a sweet animal. But having the same name could become confusing." Thinking a moment, she suggested, "How about my middle name."

"Judy?" Steve asked.

"Yeah."

"Judy, hmm. Yeah, o.k. Judy it is."

"And the orang?"

Steve pondered for a moment, "Hmm."

"He's a bit more difficult. He is slow and strong. We could call him Red," said Marti.

"Or Hairy," added Steve with a laugh. "Reminds me a bit of my brother, Curtis Jerome."

"You want to name him after your brother?" Marti asked.

"Not really. Maybe just initials? You know, 'C.J.'," said Steve with a big grin on his face. "Kinda like keeping it all in the family."

"Would your brother be upset?"

"Nah, you know him - he'd think it was funny."

"Okay," agreed Marti. "They now have new names."

In the weeks that followed Judy and C.J. slowly regained their strength. The vet came a few times to check on them and leave more medicine. Both were becoming calmer. They trusted Marti more and more. But not so the men. If one were to walk too close, they would do a war whoop and scream.

Whenever Marti went to the cage to feed them she would call them by their names.

It took no time at all before they would come to her when hearing their name.

Up to now, Marti had been hand feeding them. The apes would come over to the fence whenever she came to see them. Using a large wooden kettle spoon, she would sit outside the cage and feed them through the wire a spoonful at a time.

"Doesn't that take a long time?" Steve commented as he watched her one morning.

"Sure, but it's the best way for them to learn they can trust us. I want them to know we are not all bad people like others that I know," she said with a condescending look.

"Marti, that's not fair," he said.

"Sorry, but every time I think of what happened, well, it just bothers me."

One day, the spoon slipped from Marti's hand and fell into the cage. Judy looked down at it, picked it up, gave it a lick or two, and then handed it back to her! Marti was so thrilled by this that from then on she would see to it that occasionally the spoon fell into the cage.

Another time while being fed, Marti's attention was drawn to a commotion behind her. C.J. reached through the cage wire and steadied her hand so he could eat. It was the first time they touched.

After the 'drop the spoon' episode, Marti saw to it that they touched often. It reached a point that when she was to leave they would hold onto her and whimper. They were also becoming less afraid of the men at the ranch, especially Steve.

Marti had been called away during a feeding session and left the spoon and container of food next to the cage. Upon returning she couldn't believe her eyes.

Judy had taken the spoon, dipped it in the food container and was feeding C.J! Her timing wasn't all that perfect. Sometime C.J. would turn his head and instead of the food going in his mouth it ended up on his neck. But what a wonderful thing to see.

She wanted to yell for Steve to come and see it but didn't want to disturb them.

Then, one day, while Marti was feeding the apes, she surprised Steve by saying, "I want to go in the cage with them."

"What? No way. It's too dangerous."

"Come on, Steve, they're still quite young and not very big. How dangerous can they be?"

"Very. Look, these animals are known for their strength. If they were to get angry, well who knows what they would do? Have you looked at their fangs lately?"

"Yes but . . . well, I want to try, and I think it will help them like humans."

"Maybe women, but I don't think they will ever like men," he said.

"We know why, don't we?" she said, referring to the night the men netted the apes.

"You're always putting a dig at me. I didn't do it, other people did. And, Marti, that was a different time. The men didn't know what they were getting into, and it was quite dark, you know. You can't continue to blame them . . . or me."

"O.k. Sorry, I won't mention it again." She glanced back at the two primates, now sitting peacefully, happy and full. "But I still want to go in with them. You can be there, but far away," she said quite adamantly.

Steve knew that when she was that determined he would have to give in and so he did. Marti didn't wait long. She was afraid her husband might change his mind and she was anxious to be with the animals.

The next morning, with Steve standing nearby, Marti, figuring they were hungry for their breakfast, felt it would be the best time to go in. She had put the food in a wicker basket and the warm milk in a thermos.

She spoke to them for a while outside the cage, then causally unlocked the cage and stepped in locking the door behind her. The apes sat on the ground as they always did, waiting to be fed. She sat down in front of them, opened the basket, and proceeded to feed them. Judy held her hand as she scooped the food up. C.J. picked at a spot on her trousers a few times, Judy nonchalantly picked her nose. Both acted as if they had done it many times before. Marti was ecstatic.

In the weeks that followed, Judy's wounds healed quickly. C.J. took a while longer. As they regained their strength their attitude slowly changed, they became more trusting, more relaxed.

After her first time in the cage, Marti was able to go in and out freely. Food time became play time with them jumping up and down. A special moment came when Judy, in the middle of rough housing, jumped into Marti's arms and hugged her. That moment was a treasure for Marti. She hugged her back, kissing her on the cheek. Judy had never had that done before. Since then, it became a routine. Enter the cage, jump in her arms, a big hug and a kiss. Marti would spend hours in their cage grooming them. She would brush and comb them while they lay on their backs, arms, and legs stretched to their fullest. Even their eyes would close. Sometimes one or the other would start to snore. After each grooming they would sit up in front of Marti and wait while she took out her bottle of perfume and gently sprayed a mist over each of them. They thought that was hysterical. Judy did her chimp giggle, C.J. well, he did his thing. For the next half hour they would compare each one's odor by smelling each other's bodies. Within the next month, they had truly become members of the family.

It was a different matter when any of the neighbors came to visit. They couldn't forget that horrible experience the men had caused. They would race around the cages throwing whatever was available, screaming at the top of their lungs. Whenever any of them came too close to their cage the apes stopped whatever they were doing and shrieked. Sometimes Judy would start to shake. Once C.J. picked up a piece of car part and threw it at them.

After seeing them both clean and playing with Marti they all felt horrible. Many apologized.

"We never knew animals could be so...well, you know, affectionate."

"This is unbelievable," said Mateebi. "I can't believe these are the same two we caught in the farm."

As the months passed the apes became more accepting of different things. Trusting Steve was one of them. It took time but the first day they let Steve feed them was the breakthrough. Even Karimi was allowed in the cage to clean up. It wasn't long before they would launch themselves on his back and rough house.

Seeing their antic of rage she was reminded of what Steve had told her: As they become older they can become dangerous unless you have control of them. That meant respect for her. Although they learned to obey Marti, she was concerned that their hatred toward men might someday cause them to do something rash. Marti learned to keep a strong control on them. Sometimes it was difficult. To say no to a piece of candy or yes 'you have to' take a bath. She knew that someday there could be more serious issues than a piece of candy or a bath.

Their transition from being wild animals into domestic ones was far quicker than expected and Marti's care had built them into strong and able primates. C.J. stood four feet tall. His red hair had come in thicker and covered his whole body. Always with a sleepy wistful look, you would think he was on drugs. He surely weighted seventy pounds and was still growing. The books said he can weight two hundred pounds. What will I do with him then? Marti thought. His long arms let him touch the floor while standing up.

As for Judy, she stood three feet tall and weighed 45 pounds. Her hair was like C.J.'s, thick and jet black, and it had a shine to it. In personality she was in all ways the opposite of C.J. Where Judy was quick witted, C.J. was slow and nonchalant. The only thing they did alike was pick their nose or each other's.

Marti spent time reading about the nature of primates and discovered that they were exceedingly intelligent and they seemed to love the companionship of humans. She learned that what was important was for her to maintain an alpha position. She could never allow them to be in a superior position. Their judgment was different from hers. She knew, like children, they would challenge her on many issues. What was right and wrong? In their world, their judgment may work but if they were to live in the human world then they must obey her wishes. It was for both their safety and well-being, as well as for Steve's and hers.

Then one day, while taking their morning walk around the property, something happened that changed the lives of both Judy and C.J. The plantation had originally been cut out of the jungle. All around its perimeter was a heavy thick jungle. Although Steve had put up a fence around the property, the jungle growth had broken it down and in some cases, the foliage had crept into the plantation destroying the crops.

Their walk was something they had been doing since they were allowed out of their cage. Each morning the three of them would go on a walkabout around the edge where the fence was sometimes seen. She always brought a few goodies. Things that they wouldn't find in their lunch such as candy bars or cookies. Marti was at the edge of the jungle picking some flowers for the dining room table when it happened.

From out of nowhere, a huge python that had been lying in the tall underbrush struck at her. Being low to the ground, he bit into her boot, its long teeth going through to her leg. Immediately it coiled its massive body around her. The snake was perhaps twelve, maybe fourteen feet in length - not that big for a python but with his teeth embedded in her boot and leg, and the coils wrapped tight around her body, it was a dire situation.

She couldn't stand with the coils drawing her legs together and fell to the ground. She screamed for help but being far from the house and the workers nobody heard her. The coils worked their way up her body and around her neck. She worked frantically, trying to uncoil them. But for every coil she pulled off, others took its place.

Pythons are not poisonous. But the combination of hundreds of large teeth plus the extremely strong coils are just as dangerous. The teeth all point backward into the mouth. So, the more she struggled the more the teeth imbedded themselves.

She couldn't believe this was happening to her. Her frantic calls for help were becoming nothing more than a rasping in her throat as the coils tightened around her neck.

Both of the apes panicked. They remembered all too well the python that attacked them at the tree nest. They screamed, threw rocks and clods of dirt at it. They jumped up and down but kept their distance.

The coils were having their effect on Marti. She was suffocating. Every time she let out her breath, the coils would tighten, not allowing the next one. That was the way of the snake. Each breath brought her closer to death. C.J. made the first move. He reached up and touched the snake then screamed. He touched it again. Finally, he started to pull it trying to get it off Marti. In a moment, Judy joined in. Both were pulling trying to get it off. Their fear was overcome by their devotion to Marti. But it wasn't working.

The screaming of the apes was what brought Steve running to her. Much louder than a human and terrifying to hear.

When Steve arrived, he, with the apes, pulled on the snake. It released its grip on Marti's leg and struck at Steve missing him by inches. Marti was on the ground, her body lifeless. Steve took out his pocketknife and slammed his foot on the snake's head slitting its throat. It started to unravel slowly then fell away.

The apes jumped on it, threw big rocks on it, and dragged it around yelling and screaming. Steve picked Marti up and with the apes trying to help, carried her into the farm equipment room, swiping the big table clear and placing her where the apes were put when first captured. She was still breathing, a rasping choking cough. By then workers came running from everywhere.

"Someone call the doc! Now!" he yelled.

"He's in Goma, too far to be of any help!"

"Then get the vet – hurry!"

Some of the workers, seeing the apes, backed off, others ran in to help not concerned about them. Judy and

C.J. seemed not to pay any attention to them. Their focus was on Marti.

Dr. Berk arrived after a half hour from a nearby village. As she came to, she reached for her neck hurting from the bruising of the coils. Her body was a deep blue, red, and violet color. Each breath she took was torturous.

"Pythons don't break bones as a lot of people think. They suffocate," said Dr. Berk, as he did a thorough checkup. Blood was still oozing from the snakebite on her leg. There were a number of teeth still embedded in her leg. One by one, using a pair of forceps, he pulled them out. The teeth marks were quite deep and he had to flush each one out. Shots were given, salve was applied to sooth the sore areas.

During the doctor examination, the apes stayed with her, sometimes petting, other times sniffing her – it was their way of knowing if she was all right.

Steve, in the middle of the trauma, noticed that the apes had been touching him. In the panic of the moment, there had been times of contact. Arms brushing, body contact. And now their fear was over. Steve didn't hurt them and they had together, helped Marti.

After the doctor had finished, Steve carried her to the house and laid her in bed. All this time the two apes were mingling with the humans. Karimi ended up taking them to their cage – another breakthrough with the recognition that the man was not an enemy.

It was pure luck that Steve had heard the apes calling. They were far away and only the scream of an ape could have reached so far. Marti's small voice would never have been heard.

She was bedridden for weeks before she was able to sit up, let alone stand. She could only take short breaths. As the bruising diminished, her breathing returned to normal.

The apes' injuries, like Marti's, were healing. They had put on weight and were developing into fine specimens of primates. Steve, Karimi, Marti, and the other humans at the ranch had finally earned the trust of Judy and C.J.

When you live with someone you learn all about their life. Sometimes they try to conceal it but in time all is revealed. Such was the case when Orang and I were allowed to come into the lives of Steve and Marti Mathers

Chapter 3

When Steve and Marti Mathers moved to the Congo it was to create a plantation, a place where they could farm the land and still be close to nature. Above all they were looking forward to having children. It unfortunately, proved otherwise. Marti was not destined to have children. It was an emotional blow, one that stayed with her day after day. That is until the two apes arrived.

Human in build, sweet disposition, loving, all the aspects of a child. She fell into an imaginary life. They became her children.

C.J. and Judy became part of the household. Steve built a special cage adjoining the house. It was quite large and featured a very shallow water pond, as both were afraid of water. He added swings, rocks to climb on, and ropes hanging from the roof for them to grab.

Their cage was all that any primate could ask for. They had so much fun rolling and tumbling. Sometimes giggles, much like a human's, could be heard as they would fall, hitting the water and then racing around, grabbing the ropes, and doing it all over again. Eventually, Steve built a small door that opened into the house. When they saw it, they used it repeatedly - going in and out, even playing 'chairs' with the dining room set. Finally, Steve ended up putting a bolt on the inside so they would only come in when invited.

They became known as 'the guys,' although one of them, of course, was female.

She made them turtleneck sweaters, one red, one blue, in hopes they would know the difference; it surprised everyone when it seemed they did. When one used the other's sweater, a war would erupt, ending with one of the sweaters being ripped. They cherished their own clothes and let the intruder beware if they were touched.

Marti made them many clothes and even set-up a wardrobe closet in the house to hold them all. They prized their new closet and loved it when Marti picked out clothes -

tee shirts during the heat of the day and heavy sweaters or jackets during the cool evenings. Even dress up clothes for dinner!

Anyone looking at the closet would swear children lived there. Marti liked to see them dressed up. This is not to say that they always wore their clothes. Once out of sight of Marti, off they would come. There were many times Marti found them lying in the dirt.

"Well," she would say, "They're my children."

Although most would laugh at the statement, Steve felt she was starting to go too far with her domesticating them.

When the apes came to the plantation, the Mathers' did what others would have done. They were taken in by their cute and helpless way and cuddled and spoiled them like so many others would do.

Fortunately, they were young, far too young to cause any serious damage. They were still at the age that, if they did a boo-boo, Marti or Steve would come down on them as they would if they had a child. It was enough to keep them controlled for now.

They were allowed to eat at the dinner table providing they were well mannered, which they were. They had their own chairs, each with two cushions so they could reach the tabletop. Cloth napkins were tied around their necks that they used to wipe their mouths with. They ate with a fork, never picked up food with their fingers, and only ate the food that was on their plate. They knew that to misbehave and make a boo-boo, like sneaking food from another plate or squabbling with each other, meant they would have to leave and wouldn't be getting the choice food. They'd have to go back to their cage and eat the regular food. Not that it was bad, just different. This was rare, as they sure didn't want to miss all that good food.

Visitors couldn't believe what they saw. Some snobs wouldn't sit at the same table with them.

"We didn't like them anyhow," said Marti with a slight smile.

Big storms with thunder and lightning sometimes scared the guys so they were allowed to sleep in bed with

Steve and Marti. Sometimes they were known to fake it. When a small storm hit many miles away that could barely be heard, at the sound of a little thunder, they would beg to come in the house, acting as if the devil was after them. Once allowed in, they would scamper across the dining room, down the hall to the bedroom, and jump into the bed quickly hiding under the blankets.

Each evening after dinner was their favorite time. Marti would brush them until their hair was soft and shiny.

C.J. had far more patience than Judy. His actions were in general slower and he gave more thought to each thing he did; nothing was rushed. Whereas Judy was just the opposite. A whirlybird in action. She was a much quicker thinker and could outguess you before you even thought of it.

If you asked C.J. to put on his sweater, he would first smell it, turn it over, turn it around, probably put it on backwards or upside-down before he got it right. Judy, on the other hand, would whip it on and be waiting for something else to do.

It wasn't that C.J. was dumb, he was just slow and loved to procrastinate. One time when C.J. was offered some popcorn, he took a huge handful but ate only one at a time. Judy, on the other hand, took a huge handful and crammed the whole amount into her mouth!

It was on a Sunday afternoon while the picking of the July harvest was in full bloom that a car pulled into the yard. A well-dressed man in his thirties stepped out carrying a briefcase. The driver unloaded a medium-size suitcase out of the boot. The man paid the driver and stood there as the car drove off. Steve was the first to greet him.

"My name is Charles Brody. You were expecting me?"

Steve, thinking Marti had arranged a meeting, was polite but curious as to who this stranger was. Marti also came out to greet the man.

"Marti, this is Mr. Brody. He said he had an appointment with me - I guess, you."

"Me? No, not me."

Mr. Brody flushed red. "Actually, it's Dr. Brody."

"Is someone ill?" asked Marti, concerned.

Charles laughed. "No, I'm not that kind of doctor. PhD only. So sorry, but I was told my colleagues had arranged for my arrival here. You are Mr. and Mrs. Johansson?"

"No, I'm afraid not. They live quite a distance from here."

"Now I'm very confused. The driver said …oh well. What to do? Could you be so kind as to get me a taxi?"

Steve smiled. "Dr. Brody, to ring up a taxi, if you're lucky enough to get through, would take the better part of a day to arrive."

Marti, eying the man up and down figured he was a creditable gentleman. "Why don't you stay here for the night? In the morning, we can have one of our men drive you to the Johansson place."

"I wouldn't want to be any trouble."

"None at all," said Steve giving a nod of approval. He motioned to Billo who was standing nearby to handle the luggage.

That night, having a drink before dinner on the veranda, Steve asked Dr. Brody what his field of study was.

He set down his drink. "Please, call me Charles. Dr. Brody sounds too formal."

Steve smiled. "Okay, Charles it is. So, your PhD . . . ?"

"Is in astrophysics. I teach at the Belington University."

"Oh my!" exclaimed Marti. "What an exciting profession." Then she added, "By the way, I hope you don't mind having dinner with a couple of primates?"

"I beg your pardon. Primates?"

Steve said, "We acquired a couple of primates a while ago. Almost family now. You'll meet them at dinner."

"What? Apes? Dinner?" A small laugh erupted from his month.

"You'll be surprised. I was," said Steve.

"So, if I can ask," said Steve, "what are you doing in Africa?"

"The Johansson's are one of our major donors. I'm here to thank them and show them the advancements we've made, as well as the projections for next year in hopes they will continue their support."

"That's amazing. It's karma that you would come here first," said Marti.

"What kind of research do you do?" asked Steve.

"It's pretty basic. We're working on developing a new program that will allow us to transmit sound into the universe at twice the light years it does now."

"That's truly remarkable. Technology has come a long way," Steve said, adding a bit more wine to Charles' half-empty glass, then adding some to his own.

Marti declined when he offered her some more.

"Thank you," Charles said. "But getting back to your apes. They actually eat at your table? How on earth did you manage that?"

"It's a long story."

"Not for me. Please, I would love to hear it."

"Come inside, we can talk there," Steve said.

For the next hour, Steve went into the detailed story of C.J. and Judy, while Marti added comments from the kitchen as she busily prepared the meal. By the time the story was finished, she was as well and dinner was served.

"It's best if you're already sitting at the table when they come in," said Steve. "It will show them that you're accepted as part of the family. Let them do their usual sniffing and small war whoops. Pay them no attention. O.k.?"

"O.k."

Marti went over to the wall and pulled the cord. A small door opened and in they came. Both immediately took their assigned seats. Seeing Charles there caused a few war whoops, a smelling of his hands, and then acceptance. Food was brought, napkins put around their necks. Each picked up their fork and started to enjoy the food. A few grunts and giggles were heard but the food was what was on their mind.

"The chimp is called Judy and the orang is C.J.," said Marti.

"It's hard to believe my eyes. You've done an amazing job with them. Usually they can be most boisterous and spoiled. These are two of the finest well-trained young primates I have ever seen."

When dessert was served, Charles relaxed in his chair, casually raised his arm, and placed it on the back of Marti's chair behind her head. Immediately both apes rose up in the chairs, tore off their napkins, did a much louder war whoop and pounded the table with their fists while stomping their feet on the chair.

"Move your arm!" yelled Steve.

Charles immediately did as he was ordered. As he did, the apes quietly sat down and resumed eating.

"They thought you were going to hurt Marti. They're very protective."

"I should have known better. Living here in the house would make them quite protective. Sorry about that."

"No problem. Look, why don't we show you your room for the night. It's been a pleasure meeting you."

Goodnights were given; Charles shook hands with the apes and followed Marti as she showed him to the guest room.

Morning came early on the plantation. Cows needed milking, plants had to be checked for bugs, rot, and reseeding. Then there was plowing - so much to do. Breakfast was served out on the veranda. C.J and Judy were there early. Food was always their first thought. They befriended Charles right off. The conversation got around to his leaving.

Steve was the one who suggested it.

"Charles, Marti and I were talking about the possibility of you staying on for a while. I don't know what your schedule is at the university, if you're even married and have family you have to return to, or if you could even spare the time, but we would love to have you stay over." He looked at his wife, "You'd never have a better classroom than here, or more attentive students than the guys."

Marti spoke up. "And they really like you, too."

"As you know, I was supposed to see the Johansson's," Charles said.

"We can drive you over; spend some time with them and then come on back for as long as you like."

Charles mused, "No, I'm not married nor have family - confirmed bachelor, married to my work as they say. And, I still can't believe that all this is really happening." He looked around the ranch and then at Judy and C.J. "In fact, I could arrange to have some time away from the university. It's a most intriguing proposition, I should say. Not to mention a wonderful opportunity to relax and study the sky from a new perspective. By gosh, I don't see how I could turn it down. Yes, of course, I would love to stay on."

So it was settled. The following day Steve drove Charles to see the Johansson's. All went well as they confirmed that they would continue to be donors. Steve invited them to come and meet the apes. They agreed and said they would call to set up a time.

The days and weeks flew by. Charles became "Charlie" and 'family,' pitching right in helping with the ranch chores.

"It will cover my cost for staying here," he laughed.

Each day he interacted with Judy and C.J. Playing ball, hide and seek, wrestling. It was wonderful. Judy seemed to have adopted him as her best friend and he, in turn, didn't seem to mind.

The weeks became a month, then two. Charlie arranged for an extended leave of absence. This was a unique experience that he wanted to continue for as long as possible.

Chapter 4

Just after lunch, a beat up old Ford truck drove up the driveway and parked in front of the cage. Two men got out each carrying a gun and looked at the empty enclosure - Jac and Churney. The door was open so they walked in and began to search for the animals that lived there, but found it empty. C.J. and Judy were out in the forest with a few of the ranch hands. The men, both shabby looking, walked over to the patio. Steve, Charlie, and Marti were having tea when they approached. Steve got up and met them at the stairs.

"What can I do for you?" he asked, eyeing the old truck.

"We're here to get our apes," said Jac curtly.

"What?"

"Ya don't understand us people who live in the forest, huh?" he responded sarcastically. He raised his voice. "Ya hard of hearing?" He said it again, even louder. "We're here to get our apes!"

Steve held his temper, for the moment. "Sorry, we don't have any primates for sale. And we certainly don't have someone else's apes here."

"'Fraid ya do," Jac sneered, moving his hand to a pistol holstered in his belt. He continued, "Lookie here my friend, we had two apes escape from our place a few months back. We hear you have them. One is a chimp, ta other, an orang."

Steve now knew who these guys were - poachers. Charlie moved slowly off the porch and made his way over to Steve. He stood next to the man, holding his breath, wondering what Steve's next move would be. Churney remained silent, content to let Jac do the talking for now.

Steve said, "You have a lot of nerve coming here. Get off my property now or I'll call the police."

Jac laughed aloud. "Ha! Well, when you do, tell Captain Hardy I said hello."

Just then, C.J. and Judy came from the edge of the jungle with the ranch hands. The two poachers gave each other a knowing glance.

Churney cried out, "That's them!"

Jac said, "We'll take 'em – now!"

They made a move in the direction of the apes. It was then that the apes saw them. They yanked their hands free from the ranch hands as a scream of sheer panic erupted from both of them. They took off running as fast as they could for their cage.

Jac drew his gun to shoot them.

Marti screamed, "Steve, watch out!"

But Steve had already seen the man move. In an instant, he, Charlie, and the ranch hands tackled the man, knocking him off his feet. The gun went off, the bullet hitting a nearby tree. Churney froze as the ranch hands grabbed him, holding him in a tight grip.

Steve lifted Jac off the ground and grabbed the gun from the man before he could aim again. "Look, asshole!" he yelled. "What in the hell do you think you're doing? You're crazy." He emptied the shells onto the ground.

"That's not my name," said Jac, pulling himself free of Steve's hold. His beady eyes, bloodshot from too much alcohol, were red with hate but controlled as he glanced at the number of men standing nearby.

"Oh really?" Steve said. "Who the hell are you, then?"

"I'm Jac, and that good fer nothing over there is Churney. You heard of us?"

"Why? Should I?"

"Well, if you haven't, you will."

Charlie spoke up. "See here, those animals are endangered. It's illegal to kill them."

"Shit, man, what do we care? Anything in the jungle is free to anybody who can take it." He reached down to pick up the bullets.

"Put them in your pocket, Jac – if you reload your gun, you won't get either back," Steve cautioned.

Jac gave him a look and for a moment, the two simply stared at each other. Finally, he picked up the bullets, spit on them, rubbed the tail of his shirt on them cleaning the dirt off, and put them in his pocket. Dusting himself off he said, "These cost a pretty penny, ya know."

"I don't give a damn," Steve said. "Now, get outta here before something really does happen to you."

Jac eyed the ranch hands standing firm, almost waiting for a fight. Charlie moved close to Steve again.

"Churney, get the truck!" Jac yelled. He turned to Steve. "We're leaving now but next time there will be more of us. I aim to get my apes back so don't think I won't."

"If you come here again you may not leave alive."

Jac smiled. "Maybe it won't be me. Those are my animals and I can do whatever I want. I have a customer waiting for them right now." He yelled for everyone to hear, "Dead or alive, ya hear me? Dead or alive!"

As he spoke, Churney pulled up in the truck and moved over to the passenger side. Jac opened the door and slid in, grabbing the wheel hard.

"Keep your eyes open, 'cause I'll be back!" Before Steve could reply, he gunned the engine and, leaning out the window, waved his unloaded gun. Everyone watched as the old Ford bumped its way down and out the driveway.

They let out a collective sigh of relief and turned to help the two frightened animals, now cowering in the far corner of the pen, desperately trying to stay hidden beneath an old tarp.

Marti and Charlie carried the two apes into the house. Both were badly shaken by the ordeal. They were holding on so tight Marti had bruises on her arms. Judy kept looking over her shoulder. The minute they were set down, they ran for each other holding and hugging tightly.

Steve went to the fridge and took out a candy bar for the guys and a few beers which he passed around. He broke the bar in the middle and gave a half to each of them. They took the candy and set it down on the sofa. Both were too shaken up to eat it.

Steve sat in a chair and looked at Marti and Charlie. "We have a very serious situation here," he said. "These guys are crazy poachers, criminals, killers. They don't care who they have to shoot if it means getting their animals back."

"They will be back, you know," said Charlie. "And probably with a few other half-baked morons like them."

Marti was still shaking from the ordeal. "So, what do we do? We aren't the type to get into a . . . shooting war with these guys."

Steve paced the floor. He watched C.J. and Judy sitting together, still clutching one another. He wouldn't let anyone hurt them. "The police won't help," he said. "They want the poachers to stay in business. More money in their pockets."

There was silence among them for a long moment. Finally, Charlie spoke up. "I'm afraid you'll have to move them."

"What?" Marti was still in shock from the poachers' arrival.

"You have to get them out of here and quickly," he went on.

She looked at the two apes and then at Steve concerned. "Move them where?"

"I don't know. Maybe a zoo," Charlie stated.

"What? We can't do that! Steve?" Marti was shocked by his suggestion.

"Marti," Charlie said softly, "we have to think of their safety. At least a zoo will take good care of them."

"No! I'd rather have Doc Berk euthanize them first!"

"No, you wouldn't!" Steve suddenly snapped. "Don't ever say that!"

"At least they wouldn't be subject to a life of steel bars, bad food, and people who don't care," she said, at the point of tears.

"You don't know that."

"That's the point. I don't know what will happen to them. The zoos here aren't like the ones overseas."

Charlie had been silent, listening to Steve and Marti's discussion. He gazed at Judy and C.J. and thought back on all their experiences together, beginning with the first time they had met, and all their adventures they had been through since then. They had strangely become family. A confirmed bachelor, he had no immediate family. He couldn't bear the thought of them being harmed, either at a zoo or by the poachers themselves.

He made a sudden decision and spoke the answer to their problems. 'I'll take them."

There was stunned silence in the room. Steve and Marti looked at the man wondering if they'd even heard him correctly.

"Look, I have a dear friend in Los Angeles who runs an exotic animal center. He developed a wonderful way to handle animals. All his animals work with him and his people. They use them in the studios. Whenever a script calls for an animal to work with people he supplies them.

"This way, they will be feed the best food, handled every day. And the people are gentle."

"Well," Steve said, "it just makes sense.

"You mean split up our family?" said Marti the tears now streaming down her cheeks.

Steve said, "We could lose them permanently, honey, if we don't do something. We have to think what's best for them." He placed his arm around her shoulder. "We have three choices. Either we give them to a zoo, stay here and fight, or let Charlie take them."

Marti stood up, her face red; sweat beads were forming on her forehead. She was pacing back and forth. "Not a zoo. No. Promise me, Steve, it can't be a zoo. Not ever!"

Steve nodded. "Okay, Marti, the zoo idea is out, and fighting is out of the question. Not only is it wrong, but someone could be killed. Jac and his partner will never stop until they get what they want. And you heard what he said, they don't care if they're alive or dead. I think Charlie's idea is by far the best one. But we all have to agree."

"If I take them, you know we'll have to leave soon."

"How soon?" asked Marti.

"Like right now," said Charlie.

"Now? No, you can't leave now. Just like that!"

Marti was now starting to shake. Her whole body was in shock at the situation.

Steve went to her and helped her to a chair. "Look, honey, Charlie's right. I figure those fellas are probably getting some men together right now. The guys should leave as soon as possible."

"Wait a minute!" Her face was red with the shock of losing her beloved animals. "Steve, these aren't just animals to be shoved around from one place to another. They're our . . . children."

She buried her head into his chest. Her pain was deep. Marti had never had children. For whatever reason, she couldn't conceive. She never felt fully a woman. She wanted children so badly. They could adopt, but something deep inside the woman rejected the idea of simply adopting a black baby when her husband was white. She couldn't bring herself to have people feel that the child was not really both of theirs. It may not have made sense to anyone else, but it was how she felt. The two remarkable apes had fulfilled her maternal desires; they had become her children, their children. She dressed them, fed them, housed them, and even tried to get them to talk.

As Steve witnessed her strong reaction to the situation, he finally understood. She was trying to make them as human as possible!

"But…but… I'll miss them so much!" she said, bursting into tears, sobbing her heart out.

Judy and C.J. sat quietly, never having seen Marti like this. Steve tried to console her. He never realized just how close she was to the apes.

"Honey, I feel the same way, but what else can we do? We're lucky that Charlie's option is available to us. Judy loves Charlie. You've seen how attached she's been to him. She would love it, and C.J. would do anything for Judy. We can't be selfish about this. If you think about it - they'll have a great place to live and someone who knows them will be there 24/7."

Down deep, he too was not happy that they were going. He cared for them almost as much as Marti. He now understood just what Marti was going through. And he was as worried about her as he was about Judy and C.J. He was not a doctor, but he felt she was showing more and more signs of emotional instability. Her desire to make them their children had gotten out of hand - the clothes, spoon-feeding,

Judy talking - she was trying to fulfill desires to have children. He watched as she went over to them sitting on the sofa. She hugged them both. They covered her with kissing sounds and hugged back.

"Now look, you guys have to go, o.k.?" She was deep in the moment speaking to them as if they really were her children. "Wear your sweaters when it's cold. Eat your veggies. Don't fight with your brother."

She gently pinched Judy's lips. C.J. took her hand so she could pinch his as well.

Steve's mind was made up; she needed to see a doctor. But he knew she could be obstinate when she wanted to be. He had to think up a reason and a way to do it. Then the idea came to mind.

"We should leave for a while as well." Marti looked at him. He continued, pressing his point. "When the poachers and their friends figure out the apes are gone, they may take it out on us. If we stay, it would be putting ourselves and the farm in jeopardy."

"You really think so?" said Marti, wiping her eyes.

"Think about it, sweetie. If they come back here and find the animals gone, who do you think they will take their frustrations out on? I think sometimes you forget where we live. Inside a thick jungle - ten miles from the nearest town."

Charlie nodded his head in the affirmative. "He's right, Marti. You should get away if only for a while. There's no need to worry about the guys. They'll be taken care of."

"I know," said Marti. "I know. It's just that I hate to give those thugs so much power. They're breaking up our family and forcing us to leave our home. That's not how it should be."

Steve said with a clenched mouth, "If the police were on our side, I wouldn't leave. With their help, we could put these bastards in prison. There's no other way. We can come back in a couple of months or so."

"But we can't leave the ranch. What about all our friends? And what about the crops? Won't they die?"

"Karimi can run it. He's a good man and will keep everything going as though we were here. And the poachers would think twice about doing anything harmful while he's in charge. He would take revenge in a most . . . ugly way."

"It's a good idea, Steve," chimed in Charlie. "A sound solution to an intolerable situation."

"I suppose we could go to my mom's place in Kenya," sniffled Marti, stroking Judy's arm gently.

"No, she doesn't have room at her place, plus I wouldn't want to burden her. If she knew the truth, well, you know how worried she gets."

Marti nodded. "That's true."

Then a big smile lit up Steve's face. "I've got it! Let's just take a vacation." He looked totally surprised that he got the idea.

"You're kidding?"

"No, I mean it. Let's turn this whole thing into a positive. We haven't traveled for a long time and thank goodness Charlie was here to help us through this mess. Like you say, Marti, it's karma. What do you think?"

"Well, I don't know."

"It would be fun. We haven't been away from the plantation for quite a while - just the two of us. A second honeymoon, maybe?" He looked at her intently. "What'd ya say?"

Marti responded, "Well yes, I guess so." She finally smiled. "O.k."

Steve hugged her to him. "It'll be great."

"There's so much to do," said Marti.

Steve got on his cell phone and called his neighbor. "Kimbu, Steve here. Yeah, you heard? I know. It was rough. Listen, these thugs promised to come back. I'm not taking any chances with my family, so we're planning to leave for a spell. I'm concerned they may come back before we go. Yeah, I know. Listen, can you and a few of your men come over and help Karimi? Maybe stay until we've gone? Yeah, just for a little while. You can! Great! I really appreciate it. Good. O.k. - oh, and, uh, bring your guns, just in case."

Steve called a few more of his neighbors and explained the circumstances. A dozen responded, far more than Steve thought necessary. When the word was out about what happened, some even volunteered to stay on the plantation until the family returned, and said they would come armed, "just in case those bastards came back."

"Now that that's settled, we can all leave together," said Charlie.

"But Steve," Marti said, "If we're going on a vacation, why not go with Charlie? We could see the guys get settled in."

Steve glanced at the two apes, who by now were quietly watching each other, munching on the candy bar they had ignored earlier - as if nothing happened. They were feeling safe again with their three protectors close by.

Steve moved closer to Marti and took her hands in his. "Look, honey, this will be a traumatic change for them as well as you. We have to let them go eventually. Let's help them get a fresh start. Maybe next year we can visit them."

Steve put his arm around her.

Marti turned away, trying to hide her feelings. "You're right, it's just that . . ."

"I know, honey I know."

The evening and following morning were chaotic. Everybody was rushing around, packing, and checking crops, telling Karimi all the particulars.

The neighbors promised to load the last haul of tomatoes of the season while others said they would pick the final mango crop before they fell, getting them ready for the marketplace.

Charlie alerted his friend at the wild animal ranch as to what was happening. He was most happy to hear he would be bringing a chimp and an orang. Steve booked tickets and animal permits.

Steve, unbeknownst to Marti, made a call to his friend in Australia asking about a qualified doctor who could help her. He had chosen Australia to visit just because they knew people there who were good friends of theirs and could help him get Marti to see a doctor. Finally, the car was packed and departures were at hand. The whole staff turned out to say their goodbyes, plus the neighbors, and true to their word, they carried guns.

"Don't worry, Mr. Steve, we will take good care of everything," said Karimi.

"Be careful in case they come back," said Marti.

Karimi smiled at her. "Do not fret, Mrs. Marti; it will be them who should be careful. As you can see, we are quite ready for them."

Hugs and handshakes were given and received. A last look at their house and with tears they left.

At the airport, more hugs, tears and goodbyes.

Judy and C.J. didn't know what was happening but they felt something and were more affectionate than ever before. Marti gave them each a sugarcane toy. Her tears hadn't stopped since leaving the house. Steve had brought a box of tissues knowing it would be needed.

"Now you be good, you guys," she said. "Take care of Uncle Charlie. Train him well. He's a good man so don't be too hard on him."

Judy licked the tears from her face. C.J., in his slow wonderful way, picked at the collar of her jacket.

"Take care of each other," she cried.

Judy and C.J. were placed in a large animal container and put on a dolly. Charlie shook hands with Steve.

"Don't worry, they'll be just fine." He gave Marti a big hug and a kiss on the cheek. She couldn't talk, being caught up in the emotion. "Plan to come out when things are right. I'll have them write often," he said.

Steve took him aside for a final goodbye. "Promise me one thing, Charlie," he said softly.

"Anything."

"You'll treat them as family."

"You don't have to worry about that, Steve. I would never let anyone hurt them. I want people to see them exactly as they are and what can happen with love and loyalty like you've shown them and they've shown you. Believe me, I want them to remain as they are – open, trusting, and, I've come to regard them, well, they're almost like . . ." his voiced cracked a little, "my family as well."

Steve nodded his understanding and suddenly understood that Charlie's offer was as much for him as for the two animals. Perhaps Charlie's loneliness would now somehow be diminished. He was a good man and Steve wished him only the best.

A final hug from Marti and away he went - pushing the apes on the trolley.

Judy watched through a hole in the back of the cage as Marti and Steve got further and further away, then were lost in the throngs of people. Big glass doors opened and soon they were feeling the chill of the airport runways, vast and dotted with airplanes. Some man picked up her cage and put it on a moveable escalator up, up into the belly of the airplane. She could see other animals each in their own cage all looking out as she was, wondering about this big world they had been brought into and where they were going.

Two planes left that day, each flying in a different direction. One carried Steve, a man not quite sure what his future held, and his wife Marti whom he loved dearly. His concern for her filled his every thought and maybe, just maybe, they could find an answer in Melbourne.

The other flight had onboard a concerned and important member of the very prestigious Belington University and two primates who had gone through their early lives as no others had experienced. They sat looking out of the cage.

They had emerged from the deepest and darkest areas of the primitive world and were now on their way into the new, modern, and 'civilized' world of humans.

Chapter 5

The flight from the Congo to the L.A. airport was a long one. Stops were made along the way. All the animals in the cargo section were watered and small rations of food were slipped under the doors to last them until arrival. The birds got their seed, cats received a kennel ration, and the dogs were given biscuits. The primates received a mixed bowl of bananas, mangoes, oranges, and apples. Fresh water containers were filled in each cage by a simple apparatus where animals would receive a thin stream of water the minute they touched the nozzle. Quite efficient.

Most of the animals slept during the long flight, but Judy was restless. Couldn't sleep. Her mind took her to places she wished were lost in memory. She remembered being in the tree holding onto her mama's strong back. They were high up in the branches where surely no one could see them. She felt a shiver run through her mama's body when she looked down at those two men far below. As she peeked over her mama's shoulder, a loud noise was heard. It seemed to bounce around the jungle, awaking all that heard it.

Then, a flash of white light from below, like lightning in the sky across the veldt in the late evening. She felt a thud from something hitting her mama's body as she lurched from the impact.

Then came the memory of blood running down her mother's face, her eyes staring into space, and then falling forward as to catch a branch that was never there. Judy had let out a small scream to tell her she was afraid but her mother never reached back to comfort her. She remembered it all. As they fell, Judy waited for her mama to grab a branch to swing away from the men below.

Judy's mind was still in the moment of feeling that awful crashing to the ground as the wheels of the 747 touched down on the LAX runway awaking her from her daydreaming. She knew she could never forget. She missed her mama so very much.

The big curved cargo door swung open. The bright sunlight made her squint. C.J., always a late sleeper awoke, yawned and started his morning scratch. It was moments later that a familiar face appeared.

"Hey, guys, how was the ride?"

It was Charlie. They were so happy to see him. They did their whooping and hollering and when he opened their cage door, both jumped into his arms nearly knocking him over, hugging and smacking their learned kisses on him.

The ride to the research center took them though the greater part of Los Angeles. The international airport was as busy a place as they had ever experienced and the constant stream and loud jet engines taking off and landing made them anxious. Even Charlie was relieved as they drove north and the screeching of the planes diminished.

Charlie let them ride upfront in the seat with him. They were in awe of the tall buildings, the massive number of cars, and people everywhere. Once on the busy freeways, he laughed as they answered the big trucks' noisy engines with whoops and cries and could only imagine their perceptions of the massive traffic system in Los Angeles. Lucky for them, they would soon be in the rural foothills, quieter, gentler, and with lots of other primates.

Thirty minutes later, he swung off the main freeway and drove until he reached a small side road in the lush countryside of rolling hills, trees, and hectares of crops. He followed the road for about a mile. Then the road ended. Directly in front of them was a huge gate.

Finally, he said, "Well, guys, we're here. We're home."

The gate opened up under an arched sign that read 'Primate Research Center.' Once inside, the two apes saw rows of buildings. One was a hospital, another a laboratory, and a large building with a sign over the door that read 'Training Center.'

Farther down was a long row of large outdoor cages, each with its own indoor access, which was highly used in winter when the cold air chilled even the most acclimated of those who lived here. Even though Southern California was warm most of the year, it still was a desert, and in the winter, temperatures drop, especially at night.

The caging was made of heavy steel construction with a strong six-gauge chain-link. Each had a number of swings and play tools. There was one very large cage resembling an aviary-like structure.

"That's the play yard," Charlie pointed out. "It's much like what you had at home, only now, you might have other playmates with you."

As they drove, they saw many chimps, orangutans, and even a few gorillas, each housed in their own cages. All seemed to be quite happy with the arrangements. At the end of the row was an empty cage.

"This is your new home, guys. Hope you like it. It's the best we could do with such short notice. Oh, and we don't refer to them as cages here. They're houses or homes."

Waiting outside of their house was a distinguished gentleman, gray hair, dark suit, and sporting a neatly trained mustache. He held out his hand warmly.

"Welcome home, Charlie."

"Thank you, Tom," said Charlie respectfully, taking his hand. "It was a long yet productive trip."

"From what I've heard, you've had quite an adventure. We have a lot to talk about."

Charlie turned to the primates. "Guys, this is my good friend, your boss, Dr. Harford, Thomas Harford, the general manger. So mind your manners."

Each shook hands, C.J. first, smelling the strong shaving lotion on his hand then shaking it.

Dr. Harford studied the two for a long while, amazed at their quiet demeanor. Normally, newly arrived animals would be running round, smelling the other primates, and needing to be leashed or immediately placed in a cage. However, Judy and C.J. remained where they were, next to Charlie, patient, behaved.

"You were right about them, Charlie. It's amazing how they act. We'll learn a lot from them."

"Tom, remember, they are guests here, not subjects. What they teach us will be exactly how they are now. I promised. And, you agreed to that."

"I did and I will honor that promise. It's just that … well, they're so . . ."

Charlie interrupted, "So our new tenant arrives next week. Are we ready for him?"

"We're just finishing work on his house. I'm glad you were able to return to take part in his acclimation."

"I wouldn't have missed it for the world. From what I'm told, he's an exceptional animal, to say the least."

"Everyone's excited," Tom confessed. "Been like a bee hive of activity since we were told of his coming. Well, I leave you to settle in. We'll talk later. Good to have you back." He leaned over to the two new arrivals. "And, nice to have you here. Been looking forward to meeting you."

For the next week, Judy and C.J. became familiar with their new quarters, and adjusted to the daily routine. They sniffed and smelled with fascination the many news shrubs and vegetation within their 'house.' They met the whole staff: trainers, keepers, cooks, veterinarians, office staff, and landscape personnel. Charlie's assistant was among Judy's favorites. She was female and reminded Judy of Marti. Whatever it was, the attraction was mutual.

Her name was Bendo, an Asian woman. She was a graduate of USC and had majored in anthropology. Judy was fascinated with her long black hair that reached down to the middle of her back. Judy's favorite pastime was stroking and combing it.

Bendo would reciprocate by combing their hair, especially C.J.'s whose red hair was almost as long as hers.

Judy and C.J. were in their house when a car pulling a cage on wheels drove by. Inside was a huge chimp-like primate. He was standing up, hands clutching the bars much like what a human would do. Judy had never seen an ape that tall. She wasn't even sure if it was a chimp or some other ape. Charlie stood by, supervising and assisting to make sure the animal was treated well and comfortable in his new quarters.

It wasn't until he came to take them on their evening walk that Judy saw the tall ape again. He had been put in a special house much larger than the others had. As they walked by, Judy gave him a chimp war whoop.

"That's Oliver, guys. I think he's a cousin of yours. He came from Africa, just like you guys did. Maybe someday you will get to meet him."

The ape turned to look at Judy but did nothing. That is, not until they had passed and then a small acknowledgement, barely audible, was heard. From then on, each time they passed his house the two primates greeted each other.

One day the big ape thrust his arm through the feed slot, his long fingers beckoning to Judy. She wanted to touch his long fingers but Charlie held her back. "Not now, maybe another time."

Judy always respected Charlie's decisions - except when it involved food. She favored sweets much more than he. "Have to watch your diet, young lady," he would say.

Each visit Charlie took Judy closer yet not too close. They sat on the lawn in front of Oliver's house. One time, after sitting for about fifteen minutes, the ape handed Judy one of his bananas. She looked at Charlie, almost as if asking permission to take it. He said, "Go ahead, but be careful." Judy slowly approached the house and took the offered food. A good sign for friendship, Charlie thought.

Bendo would come and sit with Charlie and Judy; sometimes C.J. would join them, but he'd rather pick at the grass and flowers, eating a few, rather than pay any attention to the ape.

Bendo and Charlie talked of many things. Their careers, the future of primates and it usually ended up talking more about their personal lives. There was a connection between them. The kind that could last a lifetime.

"Extraordinary animal," said Charlie. "He does almost look human. Has some of our traits. Most unusual."

"Yes, very strange," she said.

Charlie said, "He was found in the upper regions of the Congo."

"I know. I've read his biographical file. Fascinating."

"You know, that's where I ran into these two. I mean, C.J. wasn't from there but Judy was. Strange we never heard of him."

Bendo said, "According to his bio, he was kept on a private ranch for most of his life. The owner was an eccentric and never allowed anybody to visit."

"Yes, but interesting that when the old man died and bequeathed him to the Center, I don't even know how he knew about us."

"Don't be so modest, Charlie. Your research is well known the world over. Stands to reason that the old guy knew his animal was different and didn't want him exploited, so it was a perfect match," Bendo said, moving her attention back onto the ape.

"Wonder why he called him 'Oliver?' An odd name for such a creature."

"No odder than C.J. or Judy," Bendo said with a smile.

In the weeks to come, Judy would holler at Charlie if they didn't see Oliver on their walks. Nothing much happened when they did see each other - an exchange of food, finger waving, and long moments of staring at each other.

One day they saw Oliver out on the lawn. He was tethered to Hales, his trainer who walked with him.

"First time out, right? How's he doing?" Charlie asked. He looked around and saw many trainers and workers watching from discreet distances. "Seems everybody's interested in seeing his response. Any aggression at all?"

"Nah, he's never shown aggression to anyone. And there's always a backup person you know. He's over there," he pointed, "with the means to quell any outburst, so if anything did happen we'll be able to handle the situation."

Oliver became part of the staff. That is to say, he learned to greet people, carry books or equipment for his trainer, share his lunch, and even don a pair of shorts and a tee shirt. All this while walking upright and striding like a man.

Charlie and Hales slowly introduced Judy to Oliver. It was pleasant enough; smell of hands, a handshake. They ate lunch together and finally ended up grooming each other for long periods.

The Center discovered just how special Oliver was. He walked on his hind feet similar to a man, had a proboscis which chimps do not have, and pointed ears like Mr. Spock.

He peeled grapes, and had long feminine fingernails due to his rarely used knuckle-walk. He had longer legs in proportion to his body, more similar to a human than a chimpanzee. He urinated in the small sump in his cage rather than just anywhere and the most amazing thing was that he held his penis, like a man. No other primate did that. It was also found that he masturbated each day. All these facts did not coincide with any other primate. People, indeed, started to call him 'the missing link.'

Within the month, he and Judy would walk hand in hand across the campus. From afar, when they both were wearing clothes, they could have passed for father and son out for a stroll. The newspapers got hold of the unusual primate living at the Center. Reporters came, took pictures, and were amazed at Oliver's presence.

An expert animal behaviorist came from Japan to take blood samples and study this profound creature. Many walked away with the feeling that they had just been in the presence of the missing link, the species scientists had been looking for between man and ape.

Charlie, speaking for the University, was a bit more reluctant to agree. "Yes, he is unusual and yes, he has some most usual traits but further studies need to be conducted before we can say, with absolute certainty, that Oliver is the missing link."

As Oliver's presence at the Research Center became more and more public, a group from San Francisco applied to the University to visit and quietly observe this most unusual creature. It was the Sasquatch group who had also been studying the Yeti myth, the possible existence of the abominable snowman. With a promise to cause no interference in Oliver's care, they were allowed to come, but with only ten members, limiting Oliver's exposure, and interactions with too many strangers. The Center, after all, was primarily research and study. It was not a zoo or circus. The group respected their position and assured them their interest was the same as theirs - scientific and, reverential. The university assigned an area where they could camp - near, but not in the way of, Oliver's home and training.

During the day, they quietly observed Oliver and his trainers interact. It was a sight, as well as an education for them as they witnessed actual research being conducted. However, the nights were enchanted and magical. A campfire was lit on the lawn, tents and sleeping bags formed a circle round it to keep warm. A few bearded guitarists with fair voices sang of the environment and the animals leaving the earth and the blight of it all.

They were not there just to see Oliver. These people were the good people. The ones who cared for the earth. The ones who spent their lives trying to convince government, the real culprits, to change their direction and help cure the problems that were destroying the earth.

"Can we save it, one and all?" they sang.

They were a mixed group: doctors, lawyers, professional people, along with waiters and waitresses, cab drivers and students. A small blonde-haired girl/child had some tears to show for her caring. Judy was there, so was C.J., each in the arms of a hopeful animal-loving person. It wasn't important that they came from different places; their hopes were all the same.

Oliver sat on the outskirts of the fire pit. He sat upright on a log as most of the others were. He wore a hooded sweater and safari shorts. His frame, as large as any other, was ominous. He seemed to be hypnotized by the flames as so many of them were.

Anyone who looked through the flames would have seen a primitive man warming himself by the fire. The mingling of Judy, C.J., and Oliver milling with the humans was mind shattering. It all worked. Why not?

Although it had a 'hippie' feeling, the atmosphere was charged with the possibility that here was a group who cared about the planet and its animals, not necessarily two-legged.

Where have all the animals gone?
Long time passing…
Where have all the animals gone?
Long time ago…
Where have all the animals gone?
Gone to graveyards, everyone one.
When will we ever learn?

When will we ever learn?

Chapter 6

Dear Charlie, Judy and C.J.,

Marti here. Steve's out and about at the moment so I thought I would take a moment to drop you a note. We are in the city of Melbourne, Australia. The people are lovely as is the ocean. We live just a few doors from the beach and at night, we can hear the waves breaking against a wall of rugged coral dredged up from the reef. I must say it has been a great relief getting away from the farm. We miss it but at the same time know that Karimi is a reliable person and will take good care of things while we are away.

I have been seeing a therapist. My goodness I had no idea how far my mental problem had gone. I see things in a different light now. Steve and I are visiting a small orphanage next week to look for a youngster to share our lives with.

How are the guys? Doing great, I'll bet. They're so wonderful. My first week away from them caused me to go through something like a withdrawal. I thought only people who smoked, drank too much alcohol, or took drugs had withdrawals. Anyhow, I'm much better now.

Charlie, Steve and I can't thank you enough for being there for them. You and they were a match made in paradise. If you need anything, please let me know. Give them a big hug for me and a goodie to remember me by. Oops! There I go again. Better sign off or I'll be back in the loony bin.

Love and deep appreciation,

Marti

PS – Steve just walked in and told me to tell you 'hi' – so hi from him. Take care.

Charlie shared the letter with Judy and C.J. over breakfast. For a moment, he thought he had gone the same route as Marti but it was all in good fun. Although they didn't understand, it made him recall the good times he had spent there. It also brought back the bad memory of the poachers. He hadn't heard anything so he figured they were gone for good. His thoughts were shattered by a very frightened young apprentice trainer rushing up to him.

"Dr. Brody! Come quick! There's been an accident!"

"What's wrong?"

"It's Gabriel. He escaped from his home, climbed a telephone pole, and will not come down. The worst is, according to the electric company, there are some very hot electric lines up there. They're on the way to shut them down but we're worried they won't arrive in time."

Charlie yelled to a nearby trainer 'take care of the guys' and took off racing, hopping hedges, crossing lawns, hoping to be there in time to somehow help Gabriel. He arrived just as the hook and ladder fire truck did.

A crowd of perhaps thirty people, some staff, some public, had crowded around the telephone pole all yelling to Gabriel to come down. Some had candy, even popcorn, trying to coax him down. Normally, food would bring him down. He had always been a chowhound but just before he snuck out of his home, he had his dinner. This was Friday and on each Friday, all the primates received a special goodie. This Friday was ice cream so he had already had the best. He wasn't about to come down for ice cream when he could have a ball zipping around jumping on the 'jungle gym' wires.

Tom, the manager rushed up. He carried a walkie-talkie. He was followed by the vet, Dr. Henderson.

"How'd he get out?" asked Charlie joining the group, still out of breath from his run.

"Don't know for sure but I think one of the new animal trainers was cleaning his cage and he snuck out," Tom told him. "You know our Gabriel is an expert at sneaking out of his home. He's done it before but never has he gone this far."

The fire captain arrived and pointed to the pole. He was a large man, with salt and pepper hair, carrying his helmet in one hand and a walkie-talkie in the other from which they could hear static and indistinct voices.

"You in charge?" he asked.

Charlie and Tom both nodded.

"What do you think?" asked Tom while Charlie continued to look at Gabriel and then back at the Captain.

"You see that thick cable coming up the side of the pole? The one painted red?"

They nodded, following his gesture.

"Well, if he touches it, he'll be fried."

"What can we do?" asked Charlie.

"You, not much. However, we're working toward shutting down the power in this whole area before your little monkey gets himself killed."

"It's not a monkey. It's an ape. A gibbon ape," Tom informed him.

"Well, keep your fingers crossed," replied the Captain, and he disappeared into the crowd.

Charlie turned to Tom. "We need to get these people cleared out. They're only making it worse, shouting and yelling like that. Gabriel won't know our voices from the others. He'll just be more confused."

"Agreed," said Tom. "I'll go speak to the Captain and see what he can do."

Charlie watched him make his way through the growing crowd and after a few words that he couldn't hear, he saw a fireman the Captain called over begin to push the crowd back. Tom returned to Charlie's side.

"He was just about to do that," Tom reported. "He's worried that Gabriel will cause a line to fall on the crowd and injure one of them as well."

"Boy, that little ape sure can find trouble," Charlie answered, looking up, concerned, at the ape on the wire.

"No kidding."

Gabriel, a three-year-old golden gibbon, was given to the Center for doing exactly what he was doing now. Escaping. When he was young, being lovable and appealing, he became spoiled by the people. They thought it was cute to see him maneuver the catch on his cage door. He had gotten out before but this time he was in a dangerous situation.

He was having a ball swinging on the loose wires and walking on the lines. He always was a showoff - sweet but mischievous. The people down below held their breath when he would come within inches of the highly charged red wire.

Charlie too was looking up when he heard a gasp come from the crowd.

Unbeknownst to him, Judy and C.J. had not listened to the young trainer and had scooted out after Charlie. What he saw gave him cold shivers.

Judy was climbing the pole and making good time. She was halfway up when Charlie saw her. C.J. sat near the bottom picking at a termite hole in the pole.

"Judy!" He screamed it so loud it came out as a squawk. "Get down here - now!"

She stopped, confused that Charlie's voice was different than it usually was. Had he calmed himself before yelling, she would have responded normally and come down, but now she was confused.

Charlie tried to control his voice. "Come on, girl. Get down." There was still a tremor in it and she knew it.

Judy started up the pole again. You could see her thinking 'What's the boss so mad at? What did I do?' She climbed to the top of the pole and finding a slab of wooden beams, sat and waited. Gabriel came over and the two sat and looked at each other. Then Judy got up and started towards the red wire.

Charlie tried to be as cool as possible. "Judy, come on, let's go home." This time he spoke in a more soothing tone. It's not that Judy didn't listen to Charlie. She was always obedient. It was the sheer panic in his voice earlier that confused her.

"Come, Judy," he said.

She turned around to go to him. Gabriel wanted her to stay and play. He kept tugging on her arm.

"Judy, come on. Let's go home. C.J., you, too. Come on."

C.J., having found whatever he was looking for, got up, and headed for Charlie. Judy, seeing this started down the pole. Once on the ground, Charlie gave them both a hug, then slipped their chains on which a thoughtful staff member handed to him.

The hydraulic ladder was slowly easing its way up alongside of the pole when it happened. Gabriel hadn't grabbed hold of the red wire but merely brushed by it on his way to another wire but that was enough. A surge of white-hot electricity arced its way up his arm and knocked him off the telephone pole.

The people down below saw the sparks flash. Saw his small body, thirty feet in the air, falling, falling, as in slow motion, turning over and over, arms flailing. Small whirls of smoke could be seen rising from the withered blackened arm. The smell of burnt flesh filled the air. A woman screamed as the men scrambled to catch the falling ape.

With all their falling over each other trying to catch him, they missed. He fell within a few feet of the crowd into a pile of old leaves and brush that had been windswept against a nearby fence. He bounced once, then twice, and then to the astonishment of the crowd, got up and started to run. Amazing! He ran upright on his hind feet, carrying his one long thin arm above his head, looking very much like a ballet dancer, the other, burnt, and broken hanging from a string of skin and flesh. A few yards from the fall, he started to stagger, knees wobbly and then fell.

Charlie was there first, behind him Doc and a mix of trainers and keepers. Gabriel was unconscious. His body limp, an occasional jolt shook his little body.

"Quick, get him to the hospital," the Doc ordered.

Once there, Henderson went to work: anesthetizing, cleaning the damaged area, amputating the little guy's hand, organizing the veins, arteries, tissue, muscle, and then a sterile cleaning. The skin and muscle were pulled over the elbow joint and sutured.

"What's the prognosis, Doc?" asked Charlie.

"This is one tough gibbon. Normally I would say the chances are slim but with his tenacity, he has a better chance to survive than most."

"Doc, how, after being electrocuted and falling thirty feet, could he get up and run?"

"I think the shock of it all put his adrenalin into overdrive. People have done the same. It's like being put in survival mode, running from the terror."

And survive he did. Two weeks later, he was walking the wire, although this one had no current running through it. Charlie had seen to it that a temporary cable was stretched from one end of the hospital wall to the other side. It worked as good therapy for him to regain his physical strength, balance, and will. With both arms held curled above his head he did his walk, run, or flip, whatever was in his mind to do. The arm never seemed to bother him. However once while eating his dinner at the table he reached for a slice of bread with the arm with the amputated hand. He stopped for a split second wondering why he couldn't reach the bread. Then a quick realization of his circumstances. The shoulder relaxed and the other arm went into action, picked up the bread and carried it to his mouth.

The 'Gabriel Incident' as it became known as, woke up the Research Center to the high risk that exists when security was not observed at all levels. Charlie made up his mind that a refresher lecture on how and what to do to keep the Center secure was necessary.

Escape was not the only issue. A few of the animals were quite vicious. Individuals who should have never had them in the first place had mistreated them. They were brought to the Center when other establishments would not accept them.

Most of the trainers were well aware of how animals respond when mistreated, but since there were new staff every so often, and in light of what had just occurred, he felt that one could never have too much safety knowledge and training.

On the day of the lecture, trainers, new staff, and even students and instructors from the University itself came to hear him speak. He was surprised by the number but happy to see their interest. The room quieted down as soon as he walked up on the stage and stood behind the podium.

After his welcome and introduction to the reason they were all there, he began by saying that when an animal grows to maturity, all that he was taught when young becomes more powerful. If he was spoiled growing up, he will expect to have his own way when an adult. If, as a youngster, he would break into a tantrum just as a human child does, screaming and pounding his fist, and in some cases breaking whatever was within reach, it followed that when that animal became an adult, it could become violent causing serious damage to property and injury to humans.

To illustrate his point about animal behavior, he gave an example of Hugo - a fully-grown male chimpanzee.

"When young," he said, "he was probably as sweet and cute as Judy was, but as all living things, he matured into a huge 175 pound brute. Totally spoiled as a youngster, he became vicious when he couldn't have his way. Three people ended up in the hospital from his rage. Now he was never taken out of his home. He was brought here for evaluation and study, but having the strength of four men, there was no way to control him. We eventually sent him to a zoo in Mexico where they promised him a good life, but I'm afraid it has probably been one of solitude."

His audience was captivated by the man's presentation. He spoke not only with authority but also kindness for the safety of both the staff and the animals. His passion for the world around him was prevalent in every subject he touched upon that day, and his reputation as an animal researcher garnered admiration from even those who were not in his field.

Charlie finished the lecture by saying, "The safety of animals is not only for our wild animal friends, it's also for our domesticated ones - dogs and cats at home, even squirrels in the park, birds in our gardens and yes, those pesky spiders who irritate us with their webs in inappropriate spaces!"

Everyone laughed.

"We want to make this a happy place – for the animals to live and for us to work. Now, let's all get back to the reason we're here."

The audience applauded, slowly got to their feet, and amidst enthusiastic chatter left the room to return to their classes or work. Doc met Charlie as he came down from the stage.

"You never cease to amaze me," he said as he smiled, bowing to the man.

"It was a good group, I thought," Charlie said softly. "They paid attention. Hopefully, we won't have any more incidents like Gabriel's."

"After hearing you talk, I think folks will be more aware of their surroundings. Let's get some coffee. I hear there's a fresh pot in the office." Charlie didn't answer him.

"Something wrong, Charlie?"

"Oh, no," he said slowly. "I was just thinking about Hugo."

"Yeah, unfortunately, there are a lot of Hugos in the world."

Charlie didn't know it at the time, but in his future, he was going to have an interesting encounter with the solitary chimp through a man named Ralph Helfer.

Chapter 7

Exhausted from all the stress related to the incident, Charlie was not happy to be awakened early in the morning.

"Hello, is this Dr. Brody?"

"Yes, it is."

"My name is Morris Gleason. I'm the Publicity Director for the San Marquis Zoological Park."

Charlie yawned away from the phone trying not to let the caller know he had been asleep. "And what can I do for you?"

"This may seem like an unusual request, but I'm looking for a trained chimp."

"Excuse me?" Charlie said, running his hand through his hair.

"Let me explain. You see, we have just completed an elaborate primate moated enclosure at our park. It's our plan to turn loose a number of primates into the facility this coming holiday. It will also be used as an entertainment area."

"Really?"

"Yes, it's a unique design. Lots of open space, a moat, so different from what they're used to. We are celebrating the 'Freedom from Cages' to open air moats. Eventually, the whole zoo will be void of its cages and only have moated areas. We are using the patriotic symbol of the word 'freedom' for the animals."

"But how can I be of help?" asked Charlie, now fully awake.

"The zoo is making a big production of the grand opening, kind of making it a holiday atmosphere and I thought maybe you had a chimp that would be able to cut the ribbon. It would be good publicity for the zoo, as well as your Center."

"Well, that is an unusual request. With all your primates, don't you have one who could do it?"

"That's the thing - none are trained. It's against the zoo's policy to allow them human contact. However, we are working on a program where some of them will be able to do a simple basic routine."

Charlie shook his head in disbelief. He wondered why most people thought animals were only there for humans to be amused by them, make pets of them, or exploit them. The Center received calls regularly for their animals to be borrowed for some event or another and nine times out of ten, they were turned down. Only on rare occasions would the Center allow an animal to make a 'personal appearance,' and that was usually at a conference on primates in order to demonstrate what the Center was accomplishing with its research.

"To be honest, Mr. Gleason, none of our chimps are trained either, especially to cut ribbons and such. That would require the handling of sharp instruments, and while primates instinctively are aware of dangers in the wild, I'm afraid a man-made tool like that would only injure them out of their ignorance of it. Not to be mean or disrespectful, but we do research here, not animal shows. I dare say, there'd be havoc afoot if one of our 'subjects' was to do the honors."

"That's a shame. Your Center came highly recommended. And it would be so appropriate to have a chimp open a primate arena, don't you think? The public adores our chimps but can't fully appreciate them the way they are now. It could open up so much more conservation in the wild for these creatures, Dr. Brody, and help other zoos to treat them more humanely. Are you sure?"

"I'm sorry I couldn't be of help. Perhaps an idea will come to mind of someone who could help you. Let me give it some thought. When is it to be held?"

"This coming Sunday. Thanks so much. I hope it works out," said Gleason and hung up.

Charlie hung up the phone, not sure of what he had just heard. It sounded quite easy but the unexpected could always happen. Besides, none of his chimps could even come close to fitting the bill. They barely responded to the research scientists at times. Most were unpredictable.

As he walked along the path on the way to his office, he passed Judy and C.J's area, stopping to watch Judy as she was totally engrained in rearranging their toys in a large wooden box in the corner. Out flew one, in went another, this one she tossed aside, that one she threw at C.J., who was sitting there watching, unaffected by Judy's ceaseless energy. Once she noticed Charlie standing near the fence, she bounded over to say her good morning.

She placed her hand on the wire fencing that separated her from the man who had rescued her from certain death at the hand of the poachers. She instinctively knew that this man would never hurt her. She felt something that first night when she visited him in the room.

Charlie placed his hand on top of her strong fingers. "Good morning, Judy. Having a fine time, are we?"

Judy answered with a familiar grunt that Charlie always knew meant yes. He watched her scamper back to the box and then had an idea.

"Judy, come here," he said.

She stopped where she was, turned around and knuckle-walked back to where he stood.

"Good girl. Say, how'd you like to spend the day at a zoo?" She nodded her head vigorously as if she understood and he laughed. "I think you would do a fine job. I'll be back later in the day to fill you in on the details."

As he crossed the lawn to his office, he thought, Am I crazy, talking to her as if she understands? Ha, I think, sometimes, that she really might.

The more he thought about it, the more he convinced himself it would be a good idea. Judy would be a good ambassador for the Center – for a day, at least. He returned Morris Gleason's call that afternoon.

"I think I've found a chimp for you," he said.

"That's great! Is it one of yours?"

"In a way, but there's a condition."

"Anything, just name it."

"I want to make sure the scissors she uses will not be real. Can you make large ones and have them so they can cut the ribbon but aren't sharp? There must be no chance she will get hurt."

"Consider it done. Our publicity department will make a pair so easy for her to use, you won't even know they work. Thank you so much, Dr. Brody. I'll see you on Sunday – be ready for a great celebration. And thank you again."

The day was Sunday and it was "Freedom Day" at the zoo. Celebration fever was everywhere. The zoo's media department had felt that turning the primates out from a cage into the moated enclosure was a sign of freedom and so they had created the idea of 'freedom day'.

The staff at the Center was ecstatic over the whole thing. They, too, had caught the fever and when Charlie was leaving for the zoo with Judy, a few of his associates emerged from around the administration building blowing horns, some wearing crazy animal makeup. It was a wonderful send off.

The two-hour ride to the zoo was quiet until they pulled into the VIP section of the parking lot. They were amazed at what they saw. Hundreds of animal lovers, some dressed in Uncle Sam outfits, some dressed in flag costumes and a band playing patriotic music loud and cheerful, awaited them. Judy got into her jig dance, stomping her feet, waving her hands and hooting at the same time. Charlie was glad he had gotten a special outfit made for her. She wore a bright red shirt, a pair of blue pants and a white beret matching a white belt. Quite patriotic. All representing freedom.

Arriving at the main entrance to the zoo gate they were inundated with dozens more screaming fans, people waving banners, others dressed as animals. Charlie was to find out that the local newspapers, along with television and radio, had blanketed the event. What a great way to celebrate Freedom Day!

Charlie and Judy walked through the main gate and, with the group escorting them, headed toward the primate site where hundreds of people had gathered to see the event. Some had dressed for the occasion by wearing gorilla or chimp outfits. Many had painted their faces with primate markings; others wore long nails and 'hairy feet' shoes.

They were delighted to see this fully-clothed chimp walking confidently beside the tall man, holding his hand as if they were father and daughter. They saw that the chimp was not afraid of them, and in fact, seemed to enjoy the attention.

Arriving at the top of the structure Charlie was amazed at what he saw. He looked down at an extraordinary animal exhibit.

The first of its kind, it resembled a Roman amphitheater curved into a half circle. Circling the front stage at the outer perimeter was a moat filled with water perhaps twenty feet wide and deep enough to dissuade any primate from crossing it. Flanked on each side were the 'mountains' which were some forty to fifty feet high on either side. There were staggered peaks, deep crevices, and sheer rock face cliffs.

The site was going to be unique since aside from being a primate enclosure, it was to be a performance area as well. When there were no shows, primates would take turns and be released onto the mountains to play and romp at will. When a performance was scheduled, the primates would be put into their housing units located at the back of the stage area and the performers brought out. Surrounding the project were row upon row of bleachers extending high up to the entrance above.

Charlie and Judy were ushered down onto the exhibit staging area. They crossed on a temporary water ramp to get into the center of the exhibit.

Waiting for them were two men, the P.R. Director and the contractor/designer. One well-dressed and distinguished, the other shabby and unshaven, still wearing his work clothes.

"Dr. Charles Brody, I presume? Morris Gleason," said the PR Director as they shook hands.

"Nice to meet you," said Charlie.

"So, this is Judy. How do you do?" he said, holding out his hand. He was charmed when Judy didn't think twice about returning the gesture, shaking his hand hard. "Boy, she's got a firm grip, doesn't she?" he observed, raising an eyebrow, impressed with her hand shaking. "We're so glad you could make it. This is Mr. Solenger, the builder and designer of this undertaking."

"Well," said Charlie, "I assume it was quite a challenge to design such a structure."

"Yeah, I guess so."

Charlie was surprised at the casual 'off handed' way Mr. Solenger threw off the comment. He just didn't sound very professional.

Standing in the middle of the 'Coliseum,' Charlie was shocked to see just how high the rock mountains really were. He thought of the builder. His attitude sure didn't match this highly sophisticated structure.

The camera crew had arrived and was setting up their gear. The crowd was growing by the minute, elbowing to see Judy. Many had pushed by the security and crossed over on the ramp.

"I guess we had better appease the public," said Charlie. He put Judy on a nearby rock so she would be at eye level with the people.

Another employee from the Publicity Department suddenly called out, "O.k., everybody, line up for pictures and autographs."

"She signs autographs?" exclaimed Mr. Gleason, raising an eyebrow. "She really is something special."

Charlie was surprised by this and a little worried that the sudden onslaught of the crowd might distress Judy. She hadn't been around this many people ever in her life but as Judy watched the hordes of humans form a line, she jumped up and down, excited, but not afraid.

Then, one by one, each handed her an item for her to scribble her name on. A pad of paper, their tee shirts, even their arms to have her scribble her 'autograph' on them. And, to Charlie's utter astonishment, she 'wrote' on each one without hesitation – as if she'd been born to it. This was a new behavior she had never demonstrated and yet she seemed to understand exactly what they wanted. She then did her geek smile or gave a raspberry for the cameras. She gave the girls a cheek kiss accompanied by a loud smack. They loved every minute of it.

The crowd was pleased and Charlie was completely taken aback by her ease with all the commotion, the flashbulbs, the music, the cheering, and the laughter. Judy's life had been a quiet one, secluded from this kind of public frenzy, yet she seemed to take to it like, well, like a chimp to a banana. Morris Gleason gave a thumb's up sign and said, "She's fantastic."

Charlie nodded. "She's full of surprises and is one of a kind, Mr. Gleason, and believe me, she knows it!"

He kept a sharp eye on her looking for any sign of mischief. Judy saw he was keeping her in focus, so she didn't cross the line. Not that she would, but there were things that enticed her to lose her concentration such as pulling a ribbon from a girl's hair or preening a child's arm by pulling out some of the short hairs. That could bring tears and they sure didn't need that. She stayed good.

A master of ceremonies arrived to keep the television viewers up to date as to what was happening. The camera crew set up their camera at the highest point so they had a good view of the entire area.

"Good afternoon, ladies and gentlemen," . . . blah, blah. He went on about the site, interviewing everybody including Charlie and Judy.

"Can we get some shots of you and the ape?" asked one unappealing soul.

"Chimp," Charlie corrected. "And, her name is Judy," said Charlie giving her the dignity she deserved.

"Sure, yeah no problem," came back the answer.

Judy did her silly pose as a geek, and Charlie strutted his new tee shirt given to him by his staff. It read; 'Save the Primates.' Judy truly loved being the center of attention. Any fear that Charlie might have had that it would be too much for her and she would cower near him at all times, quickly dissolved as he watched her interact with the crowd.

They went crazy when she took the mic and did her mumbo jumbo into it ending with a loud raspberry. For her finale, she blew up a balloon one of the people had given her. Even Charlie was surprised by this. He tied it so the air didn't leak out, then with a bash from Judy's arm, she sent it sailing in the air into the crowd that kept it bouncing over their heads. A picture of a chimp was imprinted on it with words that read: 'San Marquis Zoo.' The microphone was setup in the middle. A row of chairs was placed near the mic where Charlie, the designer, a few zoo officials and Judy sat.

Morris Gleason took the mic, welcoming all the people who had turned out for the opening of the new primate enclosure. He thanked Charlie and Judy for coming, being sure to give the Primate Center a plug. The zoo had spent a lot of the taxpayers' money on the project and he wanted to be sure that the community got their money's worth. He explained that the concept was a first of its kind.

"This exhibit, a first of its kind, will serve not only as a moated enclosure for the zoo's primates but also as an open air arena for shows that will feature performances given by humans and animals alike. On behalf of all the primates that will be enjoying this area, and the zoo staff who care for them, we thank you, the people who made it all possible. I'll turn this over to our M.C."

"O.k. This is our moment, better yet, your moment, to officially open the exhibit," spoke the M.C. His voice boomed out over a loudspeaker. The audience quieted down. "Now, Judy, it's all yours," he said, finishing off with a, "I give you . . . 'APELAND!'"

In the center of APELAND, the zoo officials had put up a large red ribbon that stretched across the area from one mountain to another.

Judy was handed an oversized pair of scissors and with Charlie's help, cut the red ribbon. A round of applause went up which triggered a response from the elephant grotto and the lion area. Trumpets and roars were heard simultaneously.

APELAND appeared impenetrable. Any primate wishing to 'escape' would have to climb over the rocky mountains and see if there was an escape route. Charlie assumed that a professional person was hired who would know the ability of the apes. APELAND had carefully been built to prevent this from happening, or swimming the moat, since primates don't swim. It was all very impressive. The designer stood close by, with a nonchalant 'no problem' attitude. There were handshakes all around.

Judy had been tugging on Charlie's hand to go play on the mountains and seeing the ceremony was over, he let her go and enjoy herself. She deserved it. The camera, seeing her climb up into the rocks and crevices stayed with her. Soon everybody's attention was drawn to her as she went higher, higher, and finally disappeared.

She reappeared again at the very top, jumping up and down giving her geek face, quite happy with herself for getting to the top. Whooping and stomping her feet, Judy gave a 'hands over the head' victory war whoop. The crowd roared and applauded her antics.

Then Charlie took the loudspeaker. "Ok, Judy! Let's go home!" his voice boomed.

Judy stopped her showing off when she heard Charlie's voice, and then looking around for a moment, disappeared into the boulders. Charlie and the whole crowd were quiet, waiting for her to appear in the center of APELAND.

When Judy appeared, it wasn't at Charlie's feet. It was clear across the exhibit, high-up at the top of where she and Charlie had started. Judy had crossed over! She had found a way to get out of the primate-moated amphitheater! The whole audience was stunned.

No one really believed what they saw. After a silent beat, the crowd went berserk. Flags waved, drums beat from out of nowhere. A voice and guitar sang a victory song. The people went ballistic, horns blared, people yelled and screamed.

The M.C. fought his way over to the director and contractor who looked very embarrassed.

"Well, how could a primate figure out how to escape this million-dollar project?" he asked, talking to both of them.

Neither wanted to respond. Then the director spoke over the loudspeaker. "There are things about the world of animals that we humans have yet to learn. I want to thank Charlie and Judy for showing us the way."

A wise choice of words.

Charlie shook hands with the director who had this strange look on his face - part disbelief, part anger. All of them made their way over to where Judy was, behind a fence where the crowds tried to get close but couldn't because of the barrier. Judy's natural instinct to be safe from the crowd allowed her to wait for Charlie to come and get her.

When all of them arrived, Morris Gleason shook Judy's hand. The designer had a sour expression on his face and again refused to make contact with the animal. Judy again gave him a well-deserved raspberry.

Seeing Charlie, she jumped into his arms and held on tight. Television reporters were anxious to get a story and plowed through the crowd to talk to Charlie. He tried to pull away, but finally gave a statement, all the while holding Judy in his arms, and soon after, with the help of a security team for protection, made his way to the car. Once inside, just for a moment, he and Judy sat in wonderful silence.

Driving home, he felt sorry for all the primates waiting to get out into their new area. But he knew in time, the bugs would be worked out and they would have their new home.

The next day in all the papers and TV were big headlines:

"APES WIN, HUMANS LOSE"; "JUDY OUTSMARTS DESIGNER"

They wearily returned to the Center and, as Charlie placed Judy back in her cage with C.J. he said, "Well, old girl, your days as a star are over. Fame is fleeting, you know. You're just an ordinary chimp once again. Like Cinderella back from the ball."

Little did Charlie know, or Judy for that matter, that this little Cinderella was about to become the most famous chimp in the world.

Chapter 8

Ivan Tors, a producer in Hollywood famous for his series, Flipper, the story of a dolphin, had called Ralph Helfer, a well-known animal behaviorist and a provider of animals for Hollywood films and television, to join him for lunch at the studio. Helfer had created what he called "Affection Training," which replaced the whip, gun, and chair of the old-school handlers with love, understanding, and respect. Ivan was a gentle person, a creative man who had quite a few successes in filming television series. Ralph had no idea what he had in mind but agreed to meet him.

The meeting was pleasant. They spoke of many things, all involved with animals. Ralph told him about his ranch and all the affection-trained animals that lived there. Within the next month, Tors came to the ranch a number of times and was quite enthralled by the affection-training program.

It was on such an occasion that he told Ralph of his idea to make a television series called 'Daktari' which meant doctor in Swahili. It was to be about a veterinarian living in Africa with his daughter. The lead character was more than a vet. He was a conservationist, a man who abhorred poachers, and would spend a good deal of his time fighting in favor of the animals. His ranch, known as the Wameru Study Center for Animal Behavior housed a number of animals that had been orphaned, injured, or given to him for one reason or another.

Each of the animals would be featured in the series. The main animal would be a chimp. She would appear in the show on a daily basis and therefore had to be an exceptional animal. An elephant, tiger, and lion would also be part of the 'family' of animals. However, there would be dozens more needed for background.

"But I couldn't do it without you and your animals. From what I've seen here and heard in the industry, you're the one who's perfected the training. These animals could do it, with your expertise. And since they are super tame and trained, the whole cast could handle them as needed."

"Well, they'll always be wild animals," Ralph said. "Never forget that. No one can ever tame a wild animal, but these animals have been affection-trained so I can provide you with the behaviors required, including the safe interaction with the cast and crew - provided they follow the rules, and listen. I know these animals and I wouldn't want to see them injured by someone thinking they are tame."

Tors nodded his agreement and then asked if Ralph would be interested in forming a partnership with him and after some deliberation, they made a deal. Soon after their meeting they went to work. Ivan would handle the production side and Ralph the ranch, trainers, and animals. The shooting was to take place on Ralph's ranch located in Soledad Canyon in Aqua Dulce, California.

The ranch consisted of about 300 acres of semi-desert landscape. A small river ran through it. Cottonwood, sycamores, and oak trees lined the shore of the river. There were areas of thicket brush they planned to use for a simulated jungle.

Landscapers came in and planted numerous plants, carpenters built what was to be known as the Daktari house. A restaurant was built to feed the more than one hundred people who would be working on the show. They included the whole crew, the trainers, keepers, administration staff, etc. Ralph had about one hundred fifty animals at the time and had plans to get more.

Early in their talks, Ralph wondered how to get a chimpanzee that could do the series. He had been given a few of the projected scripts to read and knew that the chimp would have to be of a high caliber to be able to handle the required training that would be needed.

Chimps were not a new entity to Ralph. In the past years he had had a few chimps in his collection but none would have fit the bill for Daktari. Chimps were so much like people. No two were alike. They looked different, acted in different ways, and had their own personality. Just like people. However, there was one difference. A chimp's face revealed a lot about their intellect. Acute expressions made for smart animals, other expressions denoted less intelligence. But even chimps with less intelligence could be good. They could give way to sweet and gentle loving animals.

Bright chimps could keep you on the go. They needed a lot of attention, couldn't sit still, always wanted to play or get into trouble. Yet when it was time to work, they could get the job done. To find one that had the best side of both types was not easy. Not impossible, but not easy.

Ralph went back in his house after his talk with Tors. They had gone over the new scripts and all was in place. The chimp, being a lead player was to appear in the first show. Ralph had absent-mindedly flicked on the TV; not to watch but as a matter of habit and sat down and went over the animal sequences.

Modoc, the elephant, was to be used, as was Clarence, the crossed-eye lion, Kipling, the tiger, and a number of other animals, each in a lesser role. There would have to be a training program for the more difficult roles while others only had to do an appearance or walk on.

It was then that he was drawn to an animal on the television. He had tuned into an animal program and they were playing a report on the opening of Apeland at a zoo. A man named Dr. Charles Brody was speaking with the P.R. Director of the zoo and by his side was a chimpanzee named Judy. For the next twenty minutes Ralph was blown away watching the videotaped antics of the chimp at what had occurred earlier in the day. When he watched her make her final bow by going over the top of the "mountains" and find her way out of the primate area, Ralph knew he was looking at the star of Daktari.

It was early the next morning that he placed a call to the Primate Center to speak to this man called Dr. Charles Brody.

"Yes, this is Dr. Brody, can I help you?"

For the next half hour the two spoke, each highly qualified in their own field dealing with primates. One a researcher, the other a behaviorist.

When Ralph had completed his story as well as his request to use Judy, Charlie said, "Well, Ralph, Judy's appearance at the zoo was only for one day. We here at the Center specialize in many things - none of which deal into the socialization of chimps. Judy is almost considered family here."

Ralph pressed him. "At least give me the chance to meet her. I'll know more when I see her. Look, our respective locations are pretty close to one another. I've known about the Center for a long time and would love to see it. Meeting Judy would be a good excuse."

Charlie thought for a moment. He'd never considered the idea that any primate from the Center would be used for entertainment. They were there for research. Serious research. But then again, Judy wasn't a research animal. Neither was C.J. Judy was smart, he knew that. He'd recognized her abilities back in Africa with Steve and Marti. And, as a primatologist, this would be an outstanding opportunity to see just how far Judy's abilities could take her. If she was a success, it could mean lots of publicity for the Center and the University. And that could mean hefty donations to both. No harm in talking further, he thought. They agreed to meet the next day and take the discussion to the next level.

Ralph spent the next day getting to know Charlie and Judy and was impressed by both. Charlie's dedication to the Center, its mission and especially its animals was apparent to Ralph just in the way he approached his work. Conscious of any ill-treatment of any animal, Ralph felt Charlie's methods were not too far from his own Affection-Training, only Ralph was much more 'hands-on' with an animal.

Judy impressed Ralph even more than he had seen on television. She was friendly, animated, and quite well-mannered. Ralph knew she would easily learn and master the behaviors required for the show.

It wasn't long before an agreement was reached. Ralph would learn to work with Judy and take her on the set whenever needed. In exchange, the studio would pay a fair amount to the Center to be used in the rehabilitating of primates that had come to the Center due to abuse and injury caused by various private individuals.

For the next few weeks, Ralph practically lived at the Center, even to the point of sleeping in Judy's and C.J.'s house. Formality gave way to familiarity, Dr. Brody soon became Charlie, and a friendship began.

Although he spent most of the time with Judy learning about her idiosyncrasies in preparations for her role in Daktari, Ralph found time to explore the Center. The grounds were well manicured. Flowers and exotic plants flourished at every given corner, archway and island.

Small yet attractive waterways, fountains and streams adorned the garden areas making way for an array of birds. Situated next to one of the gardens was the special house for Oliver. Not knowing his capabilities, they had built an extra strong and sizable place where he could spend his time doing the things that he enjoyed. But most of the construction was for naught, he rarely used the swinging bars, or tires reshaped and designed for swinging. Nor did he ever test the strength of the caging material in hopes of escaping.

He would rather sit and watch the staff working in the gardens, the occasional visitor being escorted around the grounds, or the birds in their antics around the birdbaths. Charlie told Ralph that after weeks of observation he believed Oliver was a thinker.

"Had he been a human, I believe he would have been a philosopher."

There were times when his mood would change. Whenever Judy came by on her daily walks with Ralph, Oliver would pull his chair up close to the edge of the house and extend his hand out in an effort to touch her. Ralph too was intrigued with him. He felt that behind Oliver's somber ways was an animal with an extraordinary mind. Perhaps more capable than most other primates.

Through conversations with Charlie, he learned that the Center had no plans for Oliver other than to study him from afar.

"All the excitement when he arrived has dwindled somewhat," he relayed. "We'd like to do more with him, of course, but funds and staff are somewhat scarce and some things had to be sacrificed. At first, we felt we could offer him much more, but in these times, well," his voice dropped, "it's hard to admit some dreams get broken." But then his mood changed and he added, "I must say though, that Oliver is better off here than where he was, that's for sure. He's got more contact with other primates, his own, and I'm happy for that."

Ralph felt they were missing a great opportunity and that the only way to delve into the mystery of Oliver was to get to know Oliver. One day he approached Charlie on the idea of taking him to his ranch where, through a special program using the affection training method, they could perhaps get to know him and eventually find out his potential.

Charlie held a staff meeting with his top administrative research team and repeated the proposal Ralph had made. There was no resistance as those attending were excited to become a part of this new and untried "Affection Training" program at the Center, even if it was only from a distance. They eagerly agreed to Oliver's relocation.

Ralph called the ranch, spoke to Frank, his assistant, and told him that he was not only going to be bringing Judy back with him, but also Oliver and had him begin to prepare a special area where this unusual primate would live. Frank promised the place would be ready to welcome both into the family by the time they returned.

Judy was everything Ralph had hoped for - courteous to people, fast learning, and above all, not aggressive. She was safe to work around.

Judy, for the first time since living at the farm, had a constant human playmate. Both Steve and Marti fit the role before but now came Ralph. The difference: Ralph knew more about her world and was more akin to understanding the likes of a chimp.

And then suddenly, there was a surge of excitement at the Center and at the ranch as the Daktari series was to start in a few days.

Ralph and Judy were ready.

Chapter 9

"O.k., where's our star? Animal star that is. You know, the chimp?" asked Tors, talking to Ralph on the phone. Ralph was at the Center finalizing Judy's relocation and packing the rest of her things.

Oliver had been relocated earlier and seemed happy in his new home. Most of the staff had been there to welcome him and help acclimatize him to his surroundings. The enclosure was very similar to the one at the Center, only larger, and Oliver acted like any new tenant, exploring quietly, watching, meeting his neighbors, listening intently to the sounds of many different animals than at the Center. The vocalizations of lions, elephants and other primates greeted him throughout the day.

Now Ralph was speaking to Ivan about tomorrow's big start and the initial meeting between Judy and the producer. "Tomorrow, Ivan, you will meet her tomorrow."

Ralph spoke to Charlie that evening at dinner. "Well, this is it - it's official - we start shooting tomorrow. You should be there for her first day on the set."

Charlie looked up from his plate. "I can't, Ralph. I have commitments here. Besides, Judy's going to be making a new home there for the time being. She's taken to 'ranch' living really well. You've made her and Oliver feel welcome. C.J. is fine here, so what do they say, 'break a leg'?"

"Well, let's hope not," said Ralph.

Ralph thought he heard sadness in Charlie's voice and understood. "So, when are you planning on coming out to the ranch?" he asked, keeping the question light. "We've known each other for quite a while and you still haven't been to my place."

Charlie laughed. "O.k., let's try for next week."

"Deal?"

"Deal."

Both Ralph and Charlie had that same gentle yet firm way of working with animals. Their only difference was that

Charlie was more scientific in his approach to the animals whereas Ralph was into the emotional hands-on approach.

Before they left, Judy jumped from Ralph's arms and ran over to C.J. who was sitting near the door of his home. They embraced and did all kinds of chimp talk. Judy didn't know she was leaving for a while, but she acted as though she did. They preened each other and played a bit. Occasionally C.J. would reach over and pull on Judy as though to say "get going" and finally she did. She would be staying at Ralph's house in the city that night and go to the ranch the next morning.

Ralph watched them interact with one another. With the new series, Judy was on her way to a new life. One of new friends, a different place to live, and a career that would engulf many new experiences.

It was morning on the ranch. The lion section was in an uproar about something or other. The Daktari crew had just arrived and was setting up for the day's shoot. Cameras were unloaded; makeup and wardrobe people were laying out costumes and supplies. The prop man had arrived early and had an array of donuts and hot steaming coffee ready to serve the sixty-five members of the crew. The animal trainers, always the first to show, were grooming the animals that were to be used that day. Among them were Mame, the camel, Clarence, the crossed-eyed lion and Twiga, the giraffe. All were brushed spanking clean. Any bug bites were treated and even Clarence's mane was brushed into a huge puffy swell of golden elegance.

Suddenly a chauffeur-driven shiny Cadillac pulled up to the newly built Daktari house. The door opened and a hairy leg stretched out to feel for the ground.

Emerging was Judy. She was wearing her khaki outfit all cleaned and ironed to perfection. The tan pants matched the shirt with its epaulets. A pith helmet sat firmly on her head. The outfit was completed by a neckerchief tied loosely around her neck.

Yes, this was definitely Judy, the star. She ate up every bit of luxury given her. Ralph was right behind her carrying her suitcase. It seemed odd that he was acting as her "second" but after all - she was the star.

A quiet came over the crew, and then a spontaneous uproar of "Judy, Judy, Judy" was heard coupled with applause. She acknowledged it by giving her geek face and a rousing war whoop.

She was a ham from the word go. A born performer. Not many primates had the tenacity to come into the human world with the energy to move forward and learn. Judy had that. Her life at the Center had given her a sound perspective of life in society. It made her ready for the outside world.

She made the rounds meeting each member of the crew, as the human stars arrived the P.R. Department set up for publicity photos to be taken. Marshall Thompson and Cheryl Miller, the two leads, were her favorites. Maybe because she worked with them more than anyone else but she was always in Cheryl's arms or Marshall's company. The three of them were inseparable.

Judy played her role as well or better than her cohorts, a talented primate made for the silver screen. Being a chimpanzee meant little to her ability to perform. Rarely would she 'flub her lines' and in fact, she usually outperformed her fellow thespians. Ralph saw to it that her everyday existence was an integral part of her training.

An hour before shooting they would go over her "lines." First, she would have her coffee. Then cereal, fruit and juice. She ate her cereal with a spoon rather than sip it from the bowl. Peel the banana instead of biting through its skin. Use a napkin to wipe her face when needed. And so on. This way she learned things that could be used when filming.

One of the trainers brought out a camp folding chair. Once opened you could read the large bold words written on the back: Judy. Under her name was a large embroidered star.

One day they were shooting a scene on the veranda of the Daktari house. The actors were all seated around the table having lunch. The scene called for them to be in a discussion about some local poachers. During the conversation, Judy had to serve them their food, pour the coffee, and put in whatever spoons of sugar they wanted. During the filming one of the actors dropped a fork. Judy looked at Ralph. He nodded to her. She got up, walked over, bent down and retrieved the fork, putting it back on the table as the conversation continued. Judy was a master at adlibbing.

Frank, Ralph's assistant, stood by watching, helping to make sure all was in order. Before he came to the ranch, he had been a cowboy. He worked at a cattle ranch and was great at roping, riding and anything related to ranching. One day while walking through the stock section, a rope came circling through the air and landed around Judy. Frank carried his rope wherever he went, roping everything in sight - including the animals. Judy took a fashion to him and was fascinated by the rope and what it could do. She would try and try again to imitate Frank, but sadly, roping was just not something she could master.

They would spend hours walking around the ranch with Frank roping camels, zebras, lions, and people, whatever was available. Judy wouldn't leave his side. They became buddies and eventually Frank was at Ralph's side in most of the shooting. His mild manner and cowboy attitude was perfect for working with animals.

Judy was trained that whenever she did well Ralph would give her a "thumbs up." Wrong was a "thumbs down." There rarely was a wrong. No punishment, just correction. Seeing as there had to be silence when they were actually filming, she always looked for the "thumbs up."

One day the scene consisted of some people leaving the Daktari house and Judy was to help one of the guests with her coat. She went into the closet and brought out a man's coat instead. This she put on the small girl. Judy looked at Ralph and he gave thumbs down. Knowing she did wrong, she pulled the coat off the girl and went back for another coat.

This time she got it right. She couldn't contain herself when he gave her a thumb up. She let out a war whoop that made everybody jump. Then, with a laugh, the guests exited. It was a good shot.

During lunch break, she would wait her turn in line holding her plate. Once at the table, she put the silverware in her pocket with a napkin and went down the line whooping loudly at the things she wanted. Certain foods were not to her liking so she passed them up quickly. Ralph helped her with her drink, usually a Coke; however, he limited them to every other meal and replaced it with milk or a fruit juice.

When you think about it, it sounds impossible to get a chimp to befriend a lion. So how did Judy and Clarence, the crossed-eyed lion become friends? It started when they first met on the set at the beginning of the show. Whenever she passed Clarence, especially if he was sleeping, she would pull his tail.

At first, he would respond grumpily, but as time went by, he started to enjoy her antics. He would lay in wait for her. She would see him crouching, then, as she reached for his tail, he would whip it away. The two would come together scampering around like two kids. Clarence was born a gentle animal. They didn't have to train him to be that way. He never even bothered to chase chickens, dogs or cats who wandered on the set.

Clarence did have crossed eyes. It bothered him only when he was quite young. No matter how careful he was, his crossed eyes would deceive him when he least expected it. He would miss his step going upstairs. Sometimes he would miss jumping in the back of the station wagon. When walking with Judy, he occasionally would bump into her, knocking her down. Judy's innocent revenge came when she caught him sleeping. She would sneak up and jump on his back. During a break on the set, it wouldn't be unusual to find the two of them sharing their lunch, especially if the dessert was ice cream.

One evening there was a close call. They were shooting late, the sun had gone down, and the electricians had turned on the huge klieg lights to light the shooting area. The shot was for Marshall, Judy, and Clarence to walk into the scene and carry out some dialogue. Ralph was holding Judy's hand and as they walked by where Clarence usually would be lying down, she reached out to grab his tail. Just as she touched it, five hundred pounds of roaring lion lunged for her! Not Clarence!

It was Rocko, a tough attack lion who had never met Judy and considered her food for the table. Ralph yanked her away just in time, or their star performer might never have appeared again. Rocko was to appear in the next scene roaring into the camera. They had never had any bad experiences where an animal was hurt, but that woke them up to the fact that things can happen.

Ralph called a meeting the next morning to go over their safety procedures. Rocko's trainer, not thinking it would be wrong to put Rocko in Clarence's area, knew nothing of Judy's and Clarence's little game and surely was not to blame.

There were times when Judy received more fan mail than some of the other actors. They answered those with a short note and Judy's handprint. Sometimes she kissed the note wearing lipstick. Adults, as well as children, wrote her, some even telling her their utmost secrets. Even other chimps from across the world sent her love letters.

Judy picked up an understanding of the English language far quicker than Ralph learned chimpanzee. As the years passed, they no longer had to talk what they called "Tarzan talk", individual words like 'sit,' 'come' and 'stay. Instead it became, "Judy, come on over and sit for a while" or "go and say hello to the woman." Full sentences where the key words 'come' 'sit' 'go' were hidden within the sentence.

They had been working for about four months straight, sometimes late into the night. The scripts called for some very involved setups and most of them required animals' performances. It was at about 9:00 in the evening when Ralph noticed Judy slumped in her chair, sleeping. He went over to her.

"Hey there, what's up?" he asked, trying to kibitz with her. She looked up at him and went back into her slump. She was in the next shot so he took her over to her trailer to freshen her up. A good brushing, some ice cream, whatever would put some life into her. But once on the set and the director yelled "action," she walked through her actions totally lethargic.

The next few days were the same. Ralph called his vet and told him about her malaise. The vet did a thorough exam of her as Ralph and the humane officer stood by.

"Well, Doc, what do you think?" asked Ralph when the vet was finally through.

"Physically, she's in top form, Ralph. But mentally, well, I think she needs a rest. A long rest. She seems worn out."

The humane officer felt the same.

"Why not give her a rest?" the vet suggested.

It had never occurred to Ralph that she, like a person, could be overworked. The only difference was humans could tell you what's wrong; an animal can only show you physically. The next day he called a meeting of the top production staff.

"Judy needs a vacation," he announced to the curious group.

"What? In the middle of our shooting schedule? Impossible!" said one of the VP's.

"Well, I'm pulling her off the productions for a while," Ralph said. He was Judy's representative and as far as he was concerned, she needed a rest.

"What can we do? We'll jeopardize the series," spoke up one of the production heads.

"What would you do if it was a major human star?" Ralph asked.

"Well, that's different," came the reply.

"Oh really?" he said, feeling the heat rising under his collar.

"How about using a double?" someone suggested.

"No, it might be o.k. for stunts but not for close-ups and places where her training is important."

"Call an early hiatus," another said. "It's coming up soon anyhow. So call it now. That way she can rest up and be ready for the start up."

"That's a thought," said another.

The studio was called, big wigs consulted, and it was a go.

Take a break.

Later that afternoon, Ralph sat with Frank and said, "How do you give a chimp a 'break'?"

"Give her all the things that make her happy."

"Really?"

"Really."

So Ralph planned a complete "letting go." Judy could sleep all she wanted, eat just about anything and as much as she wanted, and play. Lots of playing. They went to the beach. She wore her bikini. He brought C.J. from the Center so the two could visit. They had a ball throwing sand, beach balls, splashing water at the shore, sipping virgin daiquiris through straws and lying back on her lounge chair, sunglasses in place, lotion on any hairless places. Judy rested. He could tell she was glad to see her old friend.

At home, she was given the staff's full attention. She made their rounds with them, fed the stock, teased Clarence and occasionally rode in the car to the local store. Here she could pick out whatever she wanted. The weeks flew by and Ralph could see the change in her.

"What do you think, Frank?"

"She looks good as new. I think she will be ready to go back to work." The hiatus was up in a week and the top brass were anxious to see the "new" Judy.

The morning of the first day of shooting came around. They drove Judy to the location site, took her to her trailer, primped her up, and went through some behavior things. The assistant director knocked on the door.

"Judy, please," he announced.

A splash of her favorite perfume and off they went.

They took the short walk to the set amid a round of applause that rose up from the crew. She gave everyone 'the finger'- something she learned from C.J., and who knew where he had learned it. Ralph positioned her so she could see him for her cues.

"Roll camera," said the A.D.

"Action!" said the director.

The scene was simple. Judy had to bring Marshall Thompson his tranquilizer gun, pith helmet, and pack sack.

Out she came - not carrying - but wearing the paraphernalia! The pith helmet cocked on her head, gun over her shoulder, and the pack hanging off her shoulder.

The director yelled, "Cut! Print!"

There was a roar of laughter from the crew, and a very enthusiastic thumbs up from Ralph. She was back - definitely.

The new season of Daktari was on its way, only this time Ralph made sure Judy had plenty of time for a quick visit to the beach or the local store.

Ralph occasionally let her sleep in bed with him. This was one of her favorite times. He would read while she amused herself playing "human" - pulling the covers up around her neck. She worked the remote control on the TV and pretended to enjoy watching the show. She ate popcorn, one kernel at a time. She'd put on his reading glasses and slowly turned the pages as though reading. She sipped her coffee. And, she of course, would have to turn out the light. Once done, she would crawl down under the covers and sleep at the foot of the bed.

She was not allowed to leave the bed, however. Once in the middle of the night he awoke to find her ever so slowly sneaking out of bed. He was about to call out to her to get back in bed but he was curious to know what her motive was. He heard her going down the hall to the bathroom. The bathroom light was turned on, the door closed, toilet seat raised.

He heard her piddle, then the rattle of the toilet paper roll. Far too much! Toilet flushed, seat down, light out. The padding of feet in the hallway. Then a careful sliding back under the covers so as not to cause a wrinkle in the covers. The only record of her having left the bed was a wet tushy. He was astounded! It was one thing to teach a chimp one or two behaviors that they could execute at one time but the amount of the ones she used on her own that night, and in unison, and at the right time, was unbelievable. He guessed she drank too much coffee and just had to go!

Chapter 10

"Cut! That's a wrap for today. Call at 6:00 in the morning, everybody!"

It had been a busy day at the ranch working on Daktari and Ralph and Judy were both tired.

"Let's move it, girl," said Ralph, motioning to one weary chimp.

They headed over to wardrobe where Emily, the elderly wardrobe mistress, was working on her sewing machine. Judy duck-walked over to her and planted a big noisy kiss on her cheek that could be heard across the room.

Emily blushed. She was a very timid woman, and a kiss from a hairy primate like Judy caused her a very red face. She was also an expert tailor and responsible for Judy's extensive wardrobe. Judy's long arms, potbelly, and short squat feet never posed a problem for her abilities.

"Judy, now you just cut that out," she said, smiling, as she helped her out of her safari costume, careful not to let it touch the dirty stage floor. Like so many people with whom Judy worked on the production, Emily adored her. In fact, she treated Judy more like a human than a primate.

For Judy's varied appearances, she had a huge wardrobe of clothes. They ranged from silk shirts that were used when asked to appear on talk shows or join Ralph when he gave a lecture, as well as an array of safari suits, coats and jackets. Her vast wardrobe was used according to whatever the script called for. Some of her outfits were made of special light-weight cloth for the sultry and humid heat of the jungle, others for those shots in the early mornings when the December chill would freeze the generator.

Her size 14D shoes were custom made to allow for her extra-wide feet and big toe. To top it off, a company had developed a cologne especially for her. Obviously, it was meant to be a publicity stunt but turned out to be a marketable item. It was called "Primate De La Armada," and it gave a strangely unusual yet appealing natural odor.

Ralph lived on the ranch in an old style Mexican/ westernized hacienda. Built in a horseshoe fashion it surrounded an outdoor garden complete with an old stone water fountain. Most of the year, the whole garden burst with bougainvillea, and its varied colors spread across the rooftops and down the sides of the stone house. Ralph had built a "home" for Judy adjacent to the house. Although not as big as the one at the Center, it had all the necessities to keep her happy. Many times she would sneak into Ralph's room for added comfort where she could throw pillows and raid the fridge for ice cream (under his watchful eye).

With the ranch being over 300 acres, it was a long way from where Ralph's house was to where the crew was shooting Daktari. You would have to cross the lion compound, the stock section, and cut through the pond area as well as the just planted jungle to reach the site. You could take a ranch truck but still it was a long way to go.

Sometimes after a hard day's work, Ralph felt Judy was to too tired to go by Emily's to change her clothes or take the long ride to the house, especially if he knew she had an early morning shoot. There was an alternative. They could retire to her and Ralph's 30-foot luxury trailer parked nearby. Complete with all the amenities: kitchen, sofa, full-sized bed, toilet, two televisions, and a six-speaker FM system that could be tuned from anywhere in the trailer. The trailer was a great place to get away from the hectic life on the set.

The director would come every day and go over the script to be sure that the writers didn't put something in that Judy couldn't do. It was rare if they found something. Usually when Ralph looked at the script, he would add more complex things for Judy to do, since the writers weren't always aware of all her talents.

Sometimes Judy would turn on the TV and lay back on the floor with a pillow tucked firmly behind her head, something she learned from watching Ralph do it. Her favorite shows were the old Westerns, and she especially loved the horses. This was the time when she would crave a bowl of popcorn. The whole bowl would be placed in the crook of her arm and anybody wanting some would get a cold stare from her. Ralph never believed for a moment she understood what was happening on the screen but when certain figures appeared or action that she seemed familiar with, she would react to it.

There was always someone who would comb and preen her black hair. Chimp hair can become coarse and dry, so body oil was applied to enhance her coat. She would lie on the couch and close her eyes while being brushed from head to foot. Whenever the production had a shoot in another part of the county, a big truck would hitch up to the trailer and off they would go.

Whether on the set, stage, or location, Judy's prize possession was her director's chair. She carried it everywhere she went. Beware the person who sat in it unbeknownst that it was Judy's and off limits to anyone else. Talk about a tantrum!

As indulgent as all this sounded, Judy deserved it. She worked long hours under the watchful eyes of humane officers, learning her acting and cues sometimes faster than her human counterparts could.

None of this took away from Judy's unique personality. In fact, it helped. By exposing her to the many things that humans go through on a daily basis, she learned and used them in her acting. It gave her all that the character needed to act the part. The only thing she couldn't do was speak the words, but her facial expressions got the point across. Her performances were as fine as any well-studied and dedicated actor would do and her concentration was as intense as a diamond expert cutting the Hope Diamond, which was most unusual for a chimpanzee. Their attention span was quite limited and they could easily become bored.

One day on the set, an executive from the main office in Hollywood was visiting. He wanted a picture taken with Judy. He was part of the 'money people' who wielded a great deal of power. Some, like this gentleman, loved to show off their ability to control everything. He was smoking a large cigar, filling the area with its smoke and sickening sweet aroma. There was a large "no smoking" sign right in from of him but he paid it no mind. He tapped the lit end against the armrest letting the ash fall, and then proceeded to smoke. Although smoking fascinated Judy, she was never allowed to indulge.

The big shot put his arm around Judy and gave one of those toothpaste smiles while the camera clicked away. Judy kept her eye on the cigar watching the man draw in a huge amount of smoke, the tip of the cigar glowing red and then blowing a cumulus maximus cloud of smoke that engulfed everyone close to him. Having watched people smoking, Judy kept looking at Ralph for approval to smoke. Ralph kept a 'thumb down' attitude slowly shaking his head. Then the inevitable happened.

"Ya want a drag, Judy?" said Mr. Big Shot, offering her the cigar. He didn't even give Ralph a look, knowing he would be met by his strict disposition.

"She doesn't smoke," said Ralph. He spoke in a low tone not wanting to upset the big shot. Judy, God bless her, never touched the cigar, but she did give Ralph her "poor girl who never has any fun" look.

Ivan, who was standing nearby, had been watching and gave Ralph the nod to let her do it. He was coming from a different place. He dealt with these people all the time and knew they had the power to hold up production money or worse, close the production down.

"Just a little puff won't hurt her. Huh, little girl?"

It was a challenge to Ralph. They had battled before in the offices about these kinds of things. The Big Shot was never told no by anyone - until now. Whenever the script brought up something that Ralph felt was dangerous or didn't fit Judy's character, he spoke up. Most times he lost but there were a few that he won. This was not one of them.

Ralph didn't want a confrontation that could hinder the series so reluctantly he motioned to Judy to go ahead.

Judy, having watched the man smoking, mimicked his every move. She took the stogy, tapped the lit end against the armrest until an ash fell to the ground, and then put it to her mouth and sucked on it for more than she had seen him do. Little did she know not to inhale cigar smoke. She blew a great cloud of smoke into the air. She thought this was great fun and did it a few more times taking in huge gulps of smoke.

The executive was in stitches laughing uproariously. He thought it was the funniest thing he had ever seen. Then, poor Judy started a round of coughing followed by a bit of choking. Her color changed to a pale chalky white. Dropping the cigar she got up and headed for the bushes where she upchucked until there was no more. She went to bed early that night.

"She's not working today," Ralph told the director. "Yeah, you know why."

Ralph felt bad about giving in to the executive but then realized that the experience would never leave Judy. She would never smoke again.

However - she did like beer. She could down a can in one swig. Then, crunching the can in her hand, she would look for a trash can to drop it in. Always, a loud burp followed. She was never allowed more than one at any given time.

Occasionally, when he had a chance, Ralph and Judy would go into a nearby town to pick up a few things. On one particular evening, they stopped at a 7-11 store. Judy, not bothering to stop at wardrobe, was still fully dressed in her safari outfit, which included hat, shoes, and even her Ray-Ban sunglasses. Judy, walking upright, entered the store. Ralph was convinced she fancied herself quite human.

Standing upright she pulled a cart out of the lineup and proceeded down the aisle. She knew exactly what she was looking for. She even knew most of what Ralph would get. They had been at the same store many times on the way to or from the ranch. She shopped for apples, oranges, candy, milk, cookies, candy, bananas, corn flakes, candy. When Judy came to her favorite items, with one sweep of her arm, she would brush the whole lot of six or eight items into the cart. She knew the outside wrapping of each item and would take as many as Ralph would allow.

Ralph was busy getting his list. Bread, milk, vegetables, fruit, pasta, and cheese. Then they headed for the checkout line. No one seemed to notice that this safari 'person' was a chimp. Ralph thought he would have a bit of fun. He slipped a pair of gloves on Judy's hands. With these, there was no part of her body showing save for her face which sported the glasses. Judy, one by one, put the items on the conveyer belt and when their time came to pay, Ralph gave her the money.

She handed the money to the woman who, without looking up, gave the change and receipt to her. They left with Judy pushing the cart to the car.

Unbelievable, thought Ralph. Can people who work in jobs of repetition become so entranced in their job that the world around them is nonexistent?

Ralph gave Judy the car keys to open the trunk of the car and then she proceeded to load the groceries in the trunk while Ralph held the lid open. Even though the things she did were menial, she never stopped amazing Ralph.

Once in the car, he had her remove the gloves and her safari jacket so as not to wrinkle it for the next day's shoot. She sat on her favorite pillow to raise herself up a bit. As Ralph drove out of the parking area, she rolled her window down and hung her hairy forearm out the window. An old man almost dropped his cookies when he saw what appeared to be a human with a hairy arm dangling out the window. Judy gave him the finger as they drove off.

If she saw anybody laugh at her, she would give him the finger. If the bewildered victim responded by giving her one back, she would stand up in the seat and put all her effort into giving another robust big finger!

There was a scene in Daktari where Judy had to drive. Ralph went to work on it and within a week had taught Judy to drive at the ranch.

"I should say "steer" not drive," said Ralph to the director. Because of her short legs, she couldn't reach the brakes or the gas pedal, thank God. Ralph smiled.

"How the heck did you accomplish that?" the director asked, wondering if Judy could really pull it off.

"I started by putting her on my lap, just as one would do with a child. The only difference between her and a child is that Judy has a boney butt - and that makes it quite uncomfortable. But, you'll see, she did learn the principles of steering."

There were times when she was sitting on Ralph's lap and holding the wheel that she really looked like she was driving. It got people disoriented in their driving so it was best to stop. But she was a ruthless driver. Ralph knew she had mastered the wheel when she tried to run some of the trainers off the road!

Ralph had spent many years working with animals, creating stars and placing animals in movies or television shows and while their actions could be, and sometimes were, unpredictable, he found that working with people actors could be just as problematic. Sometimes worse. Especially those who were hired to work with the animals. Whether it was a snake or an elephant, some actors had a strong dislike for the animal in question. He found if they didn't particularly like them, then getting the job done could be very demanding. And sometimes Judy found herself working with that kind of performer.

"I don't want to work with that animal - she smells bad," one particularly snobby actress said. She didn't know that Judy was sprayed with a good perfume before going on a job. Even though she was told that Judy, like humans, took a bath every day - maybe two on hot days, she wanted proof.

How? Ralph thought. Maybe she could get in the bathtub with Judy!

Many times when the 'animal' had to be carried, an actor would ask for his double to do it. Imagine! Unbelievable. If the scene called for Judy to give a person a kiss on the cheek, ha - forget it.

"Call my double!" some actors would yell.

Fortunately, there were more animal lovers than not. Most people, including the actors, loved them and actually fought over who would work with them. Judy's lovable attitude won the hearts of all the actors and crews, behind and in front of the camera. Hugs and kisses all-around.

The fun part was in the makeup department when the hairdressers combed her hair or put a wig on her. Then a manicurist did her nails while the wardrobe department began dressing her in ten different outfits until the director chose one. One scene had her wearing bright red lipstick that she proceeded to lick off. Of course, then her tongue got red and Judy would stick it out so she could see the red color at the tip – Judy had a very long tongue!

Yes, the actors who loved animals won hands down when it came to who would work with them in a scene. Of course, odds did change a bit when it came to snakes, lizards, and spiders but most were good sports.

In his years of working with animals, Ralph discovered those who had a gentle yet firm attitude became the best friends to animals. Those who chose to become tough, loud, pushy, and show-offs were the ones headed for danger.

And as Judy was becoming a major star – almost a superstar – inevitably, she became as conceited as they were. An award winner in her own right, and with a busy schedule with her television series, Daktari, plus frequent guest appearances on talk shows and starring in a few major motion pictures, she was pampered more than she should have been.

But it was hard not to. If there was something she wanted and they wouldn't give it to her, she pouted with such expression, head down, chin resting on her chest, her big soulful eyes looking up at you, and her mouth puckered, as if her world had ended.

That was more than enough to get your attention and your sympathy. As time passed, the bond between Judy and Ralph grew. They spent practically all day and night with each other – both learning much about the other. Judy watched and listened to his idiosyncrasies and they came forth when not expected.

Ralph's favorite times were at home on the ranch. This was when Judy was at her best. He showed her how to vacuum (not great but passable), put dishes in the washer without breaking them, hang clothes on the line with clothespins, open and close doors with a key, drive (within reason), dress herself, and the list went on and on. Ralph continually introduced new behaviors, each increasing with difficulty and Judy continually surprised him by learning and mastering the task. Ralph knew that when young, a chimp's intelligence far surpasses a human child of the same age, until about the age of four, and then the child moved ahead.

Their bond was growing deeper with each day. Ralph would watch her from afar as she interacted with the other animals on the ranch, with C.J. and at times, forgot the horrors she had endured. Here, she was happy and healthy, well-loved, and even respected.

When a reporter asked Ralph what his favorite times were with Judy, he said, "When Judy would put her arms around me and give a hug or kiss me on the cheek without being asked. Now that was special."

Chapter 11

Sometimes when Ralph looked at the guys, it was hard to realize where they had come from. Judy, sitting in her 'director's chair.' It wasn't that long ago she was swinging from the trees with C.J. surviving day by day on whatever the jungle (and the plantations) provided. She was a very special chimpanzee, exceptionally bright and Ralph thought at times she actually considered herself of the human race. She surely wanted the benefits that humans live with. She demanded certain foods, clothes, and freedom. Hated to be confined. Probably a reminder of her days with the poachers.

Where most chimps didn't mind getting dirty, she preferred to be neat. No doubt, it was Marti's influence that got her started keeping herself clean. She had always insisted the guys cleaned up at mealtime. She had a cloth available to wipe their faces and hands.

When they took a bath, they were taught to scrub themselves and each other. However, scrubbing each other usually turned into a free-for-all. Soap, washcloth, rubber ducky - any item within reach flew in the air. Splashing each other. The bathroom was turned into a dripping, slippery, steam room.

Seeing them like this brought back thoughts of how close the danger from the poachers had been. It sent chills up Ralph's spine. Although he maintained an emotional closeness with Judy, Ralph never forgot for a minute that even though she was in all appearances humanoid, she was still a chimpanzee. They handled things differently than humans did.

It took a lot of training to have them do it our way. Ralph knew people thought that it sounded so sacrilegious and yet he knew it was necessary if the animals were to share our world. If they were to spend their lives in the human world, then they must learn our ways and abide by them. The only way to do that was to teach them and that required him to spend most of his time with them.

As much as, or because of Ralph's respect and understanding of the wild animal, he felt that bringing exotics into the human's world was not right. It was not natural. They should be left in their natural environment. But in this day and age, he knew sadly, that was just wishful thinking. In most cases, to do that would leave them to die. Their forests, jungles, and mountains were being taken over by man. Poachers were one of the most menacing animal killers of them all.

Man was on a path of self-destruction. Like a ravenous beast that engulfs all within his grasp, the land, sea, the air itself, was being polluted and destroyed. Forests were cut down to make way for social and industrial development. Land was turned into agriculture, cities, hotels, and human communities.

So many people said, "Well, it's our planet, the land is ours."

Perhaps. But was it? Was it really? What was the old adage: the animals were here first.

He wondered if there were animal lovers at the time the Bible was written. Were there people then, like today, who cared for the animals and the land? Ralph doubted it. Especially exotics. Ralph didn't think so. There was no need to protect elephants and rhinos then. No need to protect the forest. Then, who would have thought that animals even needed protecting?

Soon there would be no room for the animals. They would perish, as did the dinosaurs.

His training concept "affection training" had caught hold and animal trainers everywhere were changing over to the new and better way of working with animals. Many, who before had used the 'fear' training method, oftentimes found the humane officer at their door ready to confiscate their animals and levy a large fine against them. Some would even find a jail sentence awaiting them.

Ralph and his company found themselves quite busy. With the advent of the gentle form of training, they were breaking all kinds of records in the handling of t exotic animals.

Ralph had been asked to go on a publicity tour with Judy touting Daktari. Judy had become a household name and people everywhere wanted to touch her and, at the least, get her autograph. Tee shirts were made; caps and toys joined the multitude of merchandise items that appeared in most department stores.

Daktari was very big on Mexican television so Judy was invited to be the guest of honor at a fiesta to be held in a small town in Mexico that boasted a zoological garden and zoo. In a strange coincidence, Ralph found out that Hugo, the adult male chimpanzee, was once a resident of the Center, and had been given to this very small zoo. When Charlie heard about the visit, he was most interested to hear how Hugo was doing.

"He was a big one when we gave him to the zoo, Ralph. But troubled. Angry. At first the Center was reluctant to place him anywhere, but they were so enthusiastic about getting him. A little shy because of his size, even then. They promised him a good place to live, so we acquiesced. Wonder how big he is now."

Wanting to keep good will with the international community, Ralph accepted their invitation.

Judy was allowed to sit up front with him in the passenger section of the plane. Her fame had spread and the local airlines accepted her as a celebrity. Upon arrival, they were greeted by an attractive señorita dressed in the traditional beautiful attire of her Mexican heritage. She greeted Judy with a handmade Mexican outfit for her to wear, including a wide brim Mexican sombrero. The celebration was at its peak with a small mariachi band going full blast.

The whole town had turned out for the event. The main street was blocked off and decorated with flowers. The men wore sombreros and rode horses that sported wreaths of flowers around their necks. The townsfolk were dressed in the customary costumes of days gone by. The food was excellent; however, Judy turned away from the 'hot' tamales, tortillas, or any of the foods that were spiked with the mouth-burning chilies that made Mexican food famous.

Ralph was delighted when the zoo director asked if he would like to see the zoo. Hugo was in the back of his mind and with his notorious reputation, Ralph was anxious to see him. A camera crew supplied by the studio was following them wherever they went. Some of the visitors, laughing, dancing, and drinking Mexican beer, had joined them as they made the short walk to the zoo. As they walked, the director, in his broken English, was telling Ralph how impressed he was with his affection training. He kept saying over and over how wonderful it was to be able to work with wild animals and train them to be gentle.

"I like to do just what you do. You could teach me, yes? You could show me, yes?"

Seeing as he didn't understand Ralph's California accent, Ralph did a lot of smiling and head nodding. He was interested in seeing the zoo so he didn't want to turn him off by not agreeing with him.

The 'garden' consisted of mainly rows of cactus: saguaro, barrel, Chula, along with the giant candelabra and Joshua trees. Rocks lined the plants and paths. A few desert flowers that had sprouted up helped to brighten the garden patch.

Adjoining the garden was the zoo. A pair of massive iron gates separated them. Perpetually left open, the hinges had turned to rust due to the burning rays of the scorching sun. By the time they reached the gate, the crowd had grown to perhaps twenty people.

Once inside, Ralph was saddened by what he saw. The whole zoo was located on an acre of land much like the garden. The cages were in shambles, held together by rusty old chicken wire. A few goats, sheep, four or five llamas, tortoises, some monkeys, and one old camel, lived in their assorted areas. Some walked free. Doors to the pens were open that allowed the animals the convenience of going in and out for food and water. Rattlesnakes piled in the corner of a wooden box were cramped in the only corner where the killing rays of the sun couldn't reach them.

What Ralph did notice was that the animals were fat. None was boney or malnourished. He realized that the town didn't have the funds to build a desirable garden and zoo. But what they had, they were proud of. He felt as long as the animals were properly cared for, had enough food and water, it was just fine. The children were holding some of the newborn goats. Others held tortoises, a few groomed a llama.

Judy seemed enthralled by the whole scene. The colors, the different clothing, the laughter, and excitement the people brought were new to her and she seemed to delight in it. She joined the children playing with the animals and even tried to participate in a game of hopscotch.

Ralph was thankful that Judy had worn her shoes. The ground was scorching from the desert sun and only the occasional lizard basking on the rocks could withstand it. A big heavy box-like structure, perhaps fifteen-foot square and eight-feet high, was featured in the center of the zoo. All sides were solid except the front.

He walked around to the open side and was surprised to see a row of iron bars. The structure was obviously a large cage made out of the local material. There was something in there.

Something big.

It would occasionally bump the box causing the whole shell to move. But whatever it was hid in the shadows out of view. The bright sun prevented him from seeing into the dark box. Ralph knew it had to be Hugo.

"What's in here?" he asked.

"Hugo – the big attraction," the director replied, his voice rising an octave. He spoke as though Hugo was the only one of his kind.

"What main attraction?"

"Hugo the Great! Each day at five o'clock we feed him. People come from everywhere to see him. That's why I have asked you to come."

"To see him eat?" Ralph asked, not sure that he heard him correctly.

"Yes, of course, but also to train him - like you do your animals."

Cold shivers took the place of the hot sweat running down Ralph's back.

"What? What? You want what?"

Ralph heard Judy give a small whimper. The heat was getting to her. He saw a group of boulders about thirty feet away and slowly headed for them. Someone had tried to use them as a place to sell whatever because over them was a dingy wooden structure. Across the top of the boulders were some flat boards. Ralph saw a broken-down wagon, and didn't know whether it was meant to be an attraction or it had just stopped there a hundred years ago. Overhead boards jutting out from it formed a shaded area. Ralph took Judy over and parked her out of the sun, then walked back to the director, all the while trying to control himself.

Picking up where he had left off, he repeated, "You want me to what?"

"Señor Ralph, I see all your movies in Laredo town on TV and you are a great man. You train tigers, lions, elephants everything. So now, you train Hugo."

Ralph noticed that in his short absence, he had unlocked Hugo's cage and opened the door.

"What are you doing?" Ralph was beside himself, partly with anger at the director's senseless act and partly for allowing himself to be put in this position.

Too late. The director vanished across the yard under a torn canvas canopy, as did most of the people in the crowd. The camera crew had stationed themselves on the other side far from the action. Ralph assumed they had a good camera lens. A little man was holding a large umbrella over their heads protecting them from the sun's rays.

Ralph started to back off. What to do? The director had taken the lock with him. He didn't feel it was done on purpose but rather as a casual move. There was no way of locking the door. Ralph knew what the director expected him to do. Train him!

Ralph figured Hugo was in the box. By the actions of the people and knowing his age, plus what Charlie had told him, he figured him to be quite large and seriously considered climbing a cactus. He could swallow his pride and run or just stand and pray.

Ralph decided to join Judy. The boulders were off the ground and the old wagon offered some shelter from the sun that would help while he figured this out. He shimmied himself up on them. Judy started to climb down to come to him. Ralph yelled for her to stay.

He sat with his legs crisscrossed on the boards - waiting. The director had believed all he saw on the TV and he expected him to <u>train</u> this…this thing.

Ralph yelled to the director, "Has he been out before?"

"No, Señor Ralph."

"Has he ever hurt anybody?"

"Si, Señor Ralph."

This was not the time to explore Hugo's history at the zoo, but Ralph knew what adult male chimps were capable of. He'd never had a serious confrontation with a primate. Any person who has anticipated impending death will understand the fear that arises when confronted with the potential of having to protect yourself from physical harm. A huge hand appeared from within the cage and, using the back of its hand, the animal knocked the steel door further open.

Out came Hugo. Charlie had failed to describe him accurately. This was undoubtedly the biggest mature chimpanzee Ralph had ever seen. A good two hundred-pound male. He had thick black hair over most of his body except on the top of his head and face. There were also bald spots on his hips where he had laid often on hard floors. Adult chimps when this big resembled gorillas and Hugo surely did. He stood upright in the middle of the zoo looking like a prisoner, in for murder, who had been locked up for twenty years and just escaped.

His face was not like most big males. It was as the desert around him - dry, haggard, pockmarked, scarred from, Ralph was afraid to think what. His eyes were deep set, flakes of dry skin scales showed from beneath the hair on his body. A couple of old wounds showed as scar tissue on his legs and back. Old battle wounds Ralph figured. This animal had surely lived a tormented life. He had his choice to move toward the people, the crew or… Ralph.

Judy stood up looking quiet and solemn, totally absorbed in this big ape. It was hard to know if he was coming to see Judy or Ralph, as she was poised on the rock just above him.

"Judy, go in the wagon," Ralph ordered in a strict voice.

She looked at him and then at Hugo and slowly bent down, and climbed into the underbelly of the wagon. Ralph guessed his age at perhaps forty, a full lifetime for such an animal. Much older than most. Perhaps his hard life had forbid him a younger death. He yawned, flashing large yellow fangs. One was broken, the other short. Stubs, yet still deadly. Ralph noticed that the director was showing a bit of fear. Why? Had he done wrong? After all, he was protected by the world's best trainer. Have no fear. Ha! Hugo started towards the people. Ralph couldn't let that happen. There were women and children in the small crowd. Who knew what would happen.

"Hey, Hugo!" Ralph yelled.

He stopped. He definitely knew his name.

"Hey, big guy. Come here," Ralph said, with as much authority as his shaky voice could give.

What? Was Ralph crazy or something, but he didn't know what else to do. Hugo again started toward the people. Judy sat on the edge of the wagon nervously watching what was happening. Then with a burst of energy, she leaped off the boulder and ran to Hugo. All kinds of thoughts raced through Ralph's mind. There goes Judy, there goes the series.

Ralph yelled at her to come back but, for whatever reason, she disobeyed him. Stopping at Hugo, she sat down in front of him. She looked so small sitting there looking up at him. Hugo stood tall. You could see him wondering who in the world this creature was. Big apes like Hugo have been known to kill their kin. A whop of his arm, perhaps a bite, Hugo's life had been so unpredictable it was impossible to know his thoughts. Usually, in a confrontation like this, there would be more activity. Chimps were generally very active running around, being vocal but that was not the case.

Judy reached up and took the big fellow's hand, then stood and started to tug him in Ralph's direction. Hugo was undecided. He seemed to want to go to the visitors and kept looking over his shoulder. The visitors had stopped laughing and drinking. Why the director would do such a thing, endangering their lives, was unthinkable. Ralph couldn't believe he had that much faith in Hugo. Or did he? Ralph knew that others copied many things seen on TV. Children used toy guns, did stunts only trained professionals should do believing that they could do them as easily. The list was endless.

What the director did by letting Hugo out was, in the director's mind, acceptable. Whatever the reason, here they stood with the large primate who had been known to wreak havoc in the past and he was with Judy, a very special animal. Judy's efforts were working. Whatever she had in mind, she was bringing Hugo to Ralph. At least it took his mind off the visitors. As they approached, Ralph felt the worst was to have any form of confrontation with him. To greet him, to meet him on his arrival would be wrong. That would require a steady look into his face and could be interpreted as a challenge.

He knew from his experiences that primates were curious creatures. Curious about everything. Ralph turned away from him and made out as if he was hiding something. He pulled his shoulders down, lowered his head as though he was doing something secretly, and uttered some primate gibberish. How did I get into this? Ralph thought. This ape could tear my head off. A bite alone could do the job.

Hugo had seen him out of the corner of his eye. He paused on his way to look back at the people and then looked back at Ralph. He was deciding which way to go. Then, with Judy insisting, chose Ralph. Walking upright, a gait reminiscent of the first time Ralph saw Oliver stride across the lawn, he approached. Ralph could smell him. A thicker than air musky strong odor. Almost impossible to bear.

As he came up from behind, Ralph bent even lower and fiddled with his coat sleeves keeping his 'secret' hidden. A massive hand grabbed his shoulder and gave a pull. It almost pulled him over but he strained against it and held his ground. Judy was busy grooming him.

When an animal is busy being groomed it relaxes, goes still, some even top off to sleep. Ralph now understood Judy's method. Whether she recognized the danger of the big guy to Ralph and knowing that grooming would slow him down, Ralph would never know. But he did know it was working.

Hugo was now at his back, his hot smelly breath hitting against Ralph's neck. Ralph didn't know what else to do. Hiding a non-existent secret kept him busy. Sidetracked his mind. Hugo arched his hand down over Ralph's shoulder, his hairy muscled arm slid past his neck. Ralph immediately started to preen it. He scratched, tugged at the hair, made ape noises, picked loose dry skin, and made out he was really into it. Just like Ralph had seen it done a hundred times with monkeys and apes. It was a very special thing to do. The subordinates did it to the elder of the troop.

The breakthrough came when he started to groom Ralph. First his arm, then his head. Imagine if you can. Embraced in this King Kong of an animal's arms, totally at his mercy, wondering what next to do. Judy was continuing her grooming. She would occasionally glance at Ralph, give him a sharp 'eek' sound, and continue what she was doing. Ralph was resting his body against Hugo's. Hugo's bulk and smell were intoxicating. Then, for just a moment, he changed his position that put Ralph within inches of his face. It was then Ralph saw a different animal. His small eyes were watering; a wrinkled scarred finger would move up to clean away white foam that oozed in the corners. His lower lip drooped red saliva. As they preened him, he would emit a short but distinguishable grunt.

Hugo was not only old but sickly. Ralph had noticed a limp when he first came out of his cage. This animal had fought many wars in his lifetime. Ralph felt his exhaustion, his loneliness. He was tired. This was not the savage beast he portrayed. Ralph groomed his face and wiped his eyes that closed from the touch. He felt him give a sigh of contentment. What a magnificent beast he was. As the sun settled beneath the hills, Ralph took his hand and Judy's. Together they walked back to his cage. The keeper had placed a large bowl of fruit at the door. The evening in the desert can get quite cool so Ralph asked for a few blankets that the director brought. His face expressed his awe of Ralph. Poor man still didn't understand.

They put the blankets around Hugo's shoulders. They sat, together, eating, and preening each other until after the sun went down. As they were leaving, Ralph told the director they would be sending a vehicle to take Hugo to a hospital as he was quite sick. The director was sympathetic.

"Sí, Sí! Of course, he must stay well." He turned to his onlookers "You see, Ralph told you. This is a great man."

Once back at the Center, Ralph spent an hour with Charlie filling him in all that happened. "We have to get him out of there."

Charlie agreed and within hours, orders were given to fly Hugo out using a special cage loaned from the SPCA. Ralph left strict instructions not to 'strong arm' him.

"Be gentle," Ralph said. "Very gentle."

Looking back, Ralph thought that Judy must have known that Hugo was old, sick, and tired. She was bringing him to Ralph to see his pain. It was a small gesture, Ralph knew, to attend Hugo with the respect the animal deserved. He thought sadly that humans would never really understand and know the abilities of the wildlife on this planet.

Especially the primates.

Chapter 12

Ralph was driving along the Pacific Ocean route headed for the location site the director had picked out for their next shoot. He had left Judy at the ranch in the hands of Frank, her favorite trainer. He knew his day would be long, hot, and arduous and so it was.

He had spent the last five hours in a small hot room at City Hall with no air conditioning, defending his position in a war with the union. He was asked by the other animal companies to represent them in negotiating a fair deal with the union. But it was proving impossible. They, the union, wanted their drivers to drive the animal rigs and were unbending in their demands. Some serious negotiations were taking place. Ralph had explained to them that there were many times when an animal rode up front in the cab due to bad weather, need for warmth, safety, training, or health reasons and a union driver wouldn't be able to handle the situation.

The worst was hauling an elephant in a large semi-truck. It could prove to be dangerous. Animal trainers had special training and talent. When hauling four elephants in a full size twenty-two wheeled truck and trailer, simply going around a corner at normal speed could topple the rig. The elephants rocked back and forth and if they leaned all together going around a curve, that was 18,000 pounds leaning in one direction! It took a knowledgeable driver to be able to compensate or the wrong move could lead to disaster – for the animals, the studios, and the unions.

He explained that some of their top animal stars rode in the cab going to the studio. Some mornings, if it was quite cold, trainers turned on the heater to keep them warm. Even snakes, which are cold blooded, were kept up front for the heat. Primates, who were subject to colds, sat up front.

However, the union was determined to have their members drive no matter what the cost. Then Ralph offered what he thought was a solution; they would allow union drivers to drive as long as a trainer sat in the cab along with the driver and the animal. But on certain occasions, the trainer would still have to drive - especially in the case of hauling elephants. Or if there was no room in the cab for three due to the size of the animal, the union driver would have to go.

"What kind of animal?" they had asked.

"Well, it could be anything. We bring what the studios call for."

"Like what?"

"Snakes, chimps, leopards, young tigers, lions, we never know."

"Wait a minute, you're telling me that you need to carry those animals in the front seat and not in a cage in the back of the truck?"

"Yes, for the reasons I already mentioned, certain animals are put in the cab."

"That's bullshit." A hefty fellow stood up in the small room. "There is no way in hell I'm driving some stupid animal that could bite the shit out of me. They'd probably shit all over the place. Smell up the cab. Put them in the back where they belong."

Another man stood up. "I've been driving semi-rigs for thirty years," he boasted. "Some old elephants couldn't outdo me."

The meeting was adjourned when things turned into a yelling squabble. The head of the union ended the meeting and scheduled another for the following week, with instructions for everyone to calm down, think about the situation, and return in a composed and professional manner.

The highway wound around the Pacific coastal beach. Ralph had just started to calm down from the fighting at the union meeting when a guy in a car driving a bit erratically pulled up alongside of his pickup truck and beckoned him to pull over. Normally, Ralph wouldn't pull over for anyone, but when he recognized the man as being from the meeting, he figured he might have had a change of heart, so the minute traffic let up, he pulled into an area where they were selling fruit. The guy got out of his car and came around to Ralph's pickup. He looked a lot bigger than at the meeting.

It was then that Ralph remembered him. He was the one who was afraid the animals would poop and stink up the cab. His face was red, either from being pissed or from drinking a lot of beer. Actually, he reminded Ralph of Pooh Bear, his wrestling brown bear. The man was not coming with a change of heart.

He leaned down on the window frame. His face was as firm as chiseled stone.

"I understand your drivers are not in the union?"

"That's right. You heard that at the meeting."

"I think they should be." His face was only inches from Ralph's. "Don't you think they should?"

He moved closer, unshaven, his breath foul of beer, his voice deep and raspy. He looked like the proverbial redneck. Now Ralph knew why he had met him on the road. No witness to whatever he had in mind. This union was noted for roughing up those who didn't cooperate.

"No, not really," Ralph said.

"We pay better, good insurance and … protection."

"Protection from what?" Ralph asked, knowing exactly what he meant.

A Cheshire cat smirk crossed his face.

Ralph got out of the pickup truck and stood firmly by the man, holding his anger but not his tongue. "No way," he said. "It's just too specialized."

The big guy ran his fingernail along the hood of the truck where Ralph had just painted a nice mahogany color trim.

Ralph figured he wasn't going to get away without a broken arm or something close to it. But what to do? This guy outweighed him by a hundred pounds and seemed to be an authority on head bashing.

The animal trainers had been resisting them for months and things were getting out of hand, but trainers needed to drive their own rigs. They were already members of the trainers' union but having untrained personnel driving their vehicles was out of the question. The guy's face screwed up into a ball of sweat, anger and wrinkles.

Ralph saw his fist clench and hoped it wouldn't be too bad. Just then, a car drove up to the stand with some people to buy some vegetables. Good, thought Ralph. At least he'd have witnesses in case the guy tried to rough him up.

He saw his fist unfold. Then, in a sarcastic tone he said, "We just feel that you need our drivers to take you wherever you want to go." He clenched his jaw.

"Only if we're going to the local drive-in theater," said Ralph, biting back his sarcasm.

"Look here, animal man, I don't give a shit about your animals. Starting tomorrow, I want to see a union driver behind the wheel on your next job - capeesh?" He thrust his thick finger into Ralph's chest. It caught him off guard. He stumbled backward and caught himself before hitting the ground. "Tomorrow, ya hear me?"

And he headed for his car. Ralph had heard for many years how certain unions, to put it delicately, were controlled by organized crime, and those who didn't cooperate felt their wrath. Getting in his truck, Ralph's drive to the studio location was filled with thoughts of how to get through this.

That evening he gathered his trainers to talk over tomorrow's problem. It wasn't that they were anti-union. Unions had helped many poor people. They were organized, paid good wages, and some provided medical insurance.

But Ralph had heard the union wanted to take a piece of the action from the drivers' payroll and that's why they wanted them to drive. With another man on payroll, it would raise the cost of renting an animal (even a mouse) and the studios were not about to increase their budgets. It was enough that they had to pay for a trainer, vehicle, and the animal. Adding on another driver just didn't make much sense. It was unacceptable.

Even now, the small animal companies were suffering from little or no work. Some went out of business. It made the cost of renting an animal prohibitive. Sometimes two or three vehicles would be required. That meant more drivers, and many times they had to be on duty for a week according to the needs of the script. The cost of production would rise significantly higher. But none of this was what worried him. Some of the studios had called saying they had to join the union or they couldn't work at the studio. Being that they were unionized, their contract stated that any affiliates they hired must be union as well.

"What's on call for tomorrow?" Ralph asked.

Frank read the list. "Two large snakes, one highly trained chimp, and a dozen geese."

Ralph thought for a moment. "Oh really, hmm? I've got an idea."

Morning came. At the ranch's main gate stood a group of union men.

Ralph noticed they had different items in their hands. Clubs, a steel rod, a wooden 2x4. A rather large man wearing a white shirt with the words 'UNION 741' embossed over the breast pocket stood at the door to the truck. His cap also boasted in big red letters; 'UNION 741.'

They sure want us to know they're here, Ralph thought.

Six or seven of the trainers and keepers had gathered around Ralph. It was obvious that if there were to be a fight, the ranch wouldn't go down easily.

"They're not going to let our vehicles leave the ranch without one of their men driving them," stated one of the keepers.

Ralph noticed a few of the trainers had brought out their favorite animals. The feeling was that they would make the union people afraid to challenge the trainers. Robert had Jojo, the leopard, Harry, his wrestling bear, Bo, and Ted had Serang, the tiger. All were trained to attack but the problem was they would go for someone, knock him down, grab his arm in their mouth, and then - lick their face! The attacks were for the camera and none of the animals would ever hurt anyone. The animals were lovers, not fighters. Of course, those men at the gate with their menacing demeanor and clubs didn't know that.

"Hey you! You're the boss, aren't you?" asked the guy standing near the truck.

"How did you get in?" asked Ralph, ignoring his question.

"We have our ways," he said.

Ralph figured that at least one of his people had already favored the union. He began helping Frank load the truck and, trying to remain calm, asked, "What can I do for you?"

"I'm here to drive your truck."

He was one of those guys with a beer belly who found it hard to sit behind the wheel. He had on a union tee shirt and baseball cap worn backward on his head. He stood, hands on hips, arrogant and ready for anything.

"Well, so you're here to drive, are you?" Ralph stayed nonchalant. He spoke to Frank. "O.k. Let's load up."

Frank gestured to a few of the men. Out came a couple of the keepers herding a bunch of geese.

"Get them in the back of the truck!" yelled Frank.

Ralph could see a smirk form across the union guy's face. He was happy to see the domestic birds were being put in the back of the truck. With this, he climbed into the cab behind the wheel, sure that all was well. He gestured a thumbs up to the men at the gate who all waved and smiled back. Some started to leave.

As the union man got settled in, the other door opened up and Judy came in and sat alongside the driver.

"What the shit? Get that mother fu.. outta here. I'm not driving with 'it' sitting here."

Ralph figured as much. "So, let me drive," he said.

The driver looked at him with hate in his eyes. "I know what you're doing. You think this will keep me from driving."

"Will it?"

"Look, just keep him over there," he said, pointing to the other side of the cab.

"Yeah, sure," Ralph said, as though he would.

At the same time, another trainer walked up with Astaroth, the twelve-foot python draped around his neck.

"Where should I put him, boss?"

"In that bag," Ralph answered, pointing to a large burlap bag in the back of the truck. "I'll turn on the heater to keep him warm," Ralph said with a tongue in cheek look. Judy, who had long ago been conditioned to work with reptiles, held the bag while Frank lowered the snake in.

"You're gonna put him in here? No fuc…ing way."

"Look, my friend," said Ralph in a stern voice. "These animals have to be at the studio in one hour. If they don't get there on time, they could levy a fine of up to $25,000.00 dollars for holding up production. Now, if you're the one who causes the delay, then you and your union will pay it, so if you're going to drive, let's go!"

The driver was in a state of panic.

"Move over, Judy," said Ralph. "You're taking all the room." With this, he gave her a gentle shove that pushed her practically in the lap of the driver.

Then the bag with the snake was put on Judy and Ralph's lap.

Frank hopped into the back of the truck.

Let's go," said Ralph nonchalantly.

The gate opened and off they went past the union guys, their baseball bats, and other weapons. Some stood with their mouths open in a state of shock but no more than the driver himself.

"What's your name?" asked Ralph.

"Huh?"

"Your name?"

The poor man was beside himself, eyes staring straight ahead.

"Joe, it's Joe."

He was driving crazy. He wanted to get to the studio as fast as he could.

"Better slow down or a cop will pull you over. I understand if a union driver gets a ticket it goes against his seniority."

Joe slowed down. He was sweating and kept wriggling in his seat. Judy reached up and turned on the radio.

"What…what's she doing?"

"She likes music."

About fifteen minutes into the drive, Judy reached over and put her hand on Joe's head.

"Oh! Shit. What's happening?"

"She likes you. She's preening."

"What's that?"

"She's looking for lice, dry skin, or whatever else she can find."

Joe heard a smacking sound. "Now what?"

"She's eating them."

"What?"

"Yeah. That's what they do."

"Tell her to keep her damn hands to herself."

"You tell her."

The driver was sweating, his hands shaking. They were swerving back and forth on the country road. He kept pushing Judy's hand away but she was insistent.

"I wouldn't get her mad. When primates groom they are totally focused. I've seen them drool and even salivate as they become so intense on what they're doing."

Joe took a hard right, causing Judy to grab his thigh. He freaked. "Agh! Tell her to get her hand off me!"

"You tell her."

"Yeah, right. It's like telling King Kong to stop molesting Jane. Get her hand off my leg."

"You get it off."

"You mean touch her?"

"Yep! Go ahead, she won't mind."

Joe reached down and grabbed what he thought was Judy. He squeezed hard in an attempt to push her away. Something was moving in his hand. He screamed. He had grabbed the snake in the bag on her lap. He pulled his hand away letting go of the steering wheel.

"Grab the wheel!" Ralph yelled.

The truck swerved almost leaving the roadbed.

"Ick. Agh! Holy shit! Yuck. Disgusting!"

Judy was still clinging to Joe's leg. Joe pushed her hand hard with the back of his hand in hopes of dislodging hers. But it just made her hang on all the tighter. He was in a near state of panic, took a deep breath, and grabbing her hand, tried to muscle it off his leg.

"I wouldn't do that if I were you, Joe - you'll tick her off."

He tried again to dislodge her. She was too strong and wouldn't let go. This time she clenched harder. By the third time he tried, she got pissed, stood up in the cab, and did her nerve chilling war whoop. Arms waving in the air, mouth open, fangs showing, feet stomping - it was enough to scare the pants off anyone not familiar with her antics.

That did it. Joe wanted off the road.

"She's attacking! Get her off me!"

"You stop her. I told you not to piss her off."

The truck came to a screeching, skidding stop. Joe was out of the cab and hit the dirt hard. Half running, slipping and sliding, he landed in a small bush area where he fell into a breathless heap.

"O.k., you win. You drive; I'll sit in the back with the geese."

Joe went to get up.

"You pissed your pants, man."

Joe looked down. "Oh! Shit, now what'll I do? I can't go to the studio like this."

In a matter of minutes, Ralph saw a tough man become a normal but scared person. The hard-hitting attitude was gone. What a difference.

"You wouldn't tell anybody about this. Will ya?"

"Suuure, we won't," he murmured.

Ralph gave him a pair of keepers' overalls to wear. They drove into the studio with Joe in the back, geese honking, feathers flying. Frank laughed as Joe kept one on his lap until he got to wardrobe.

Ralph settled the union matter by allowing the animal trainers to drive as long as they joined the union.

Chapter 13

They had just finished shooting the final episode on Daktari for the season and were putting together plans for a public relations tour. All of the stars of the series were called away to shoot in different locations according to the wishes of the head of the P.R. Department. Stories were made up and used in glamour magazines, TV spots - wherever the Publicity Department felt it would benefit the productions.

Marshall Thompson was sent up to Snow Valley, a beautiful location surrounded by a bevy of beautiful women. Cheryl Miller went to a Western ranch where they had her simulating roping cows, riding horses, and of course, always with a handsome cowboy at her side.

Judy was no exception. Being considered a lead in the series, the P.R. Department thought a love interest for her would be just what her fans would want to see so they called for her to have a love interest as well. Ralph spoke to Charlie to see if he had a large male chimp that could become her suitor for a day.

He thought for a while going over his entire inventory. "Actually, no," he said to Ralph's surprise. "All our chimps are either quite young or too old. Some are aggressive but a large older chimp that is trustworthy, I'm afraid not. You know, Ralph, Judy is an extremely rare chimp. It's because of her life living with humans, being firmly handled by people knowing what they were doing that has made her who she is today. You won't find another like her."

"But I don't need a highly trained chimp, just one who will pose with her and isn't dangerous," said Ralph, getting a little concerned about not finding a chimp.

"But you have to be careful. People don't realize the potential danger a of chimp, especially an older one."

"I know, Charlie, and you're right. Chimps sometimes revert to their primitive instincts. They can kill, maim, and destroy property in the blink of an eye. Well, so what to do?"

"I'll check around."

About a week later, Ralph remembered a couple who once had a chimp, Jerry, but that was years ago. Either they got rid of him or if they still had him, he would be pretty large by now. The owner's name was Jack Sutton, who owned a restaurant in the San Fernando Valley just outside of LA.

Ralph recalled the chimp being raised in the house with Jack and his wife, Mae. They had raised him since he was a baby and considered him a member of the family. Ralph remembered the chimp to be quite nice and the Suttons were training him rather well.

He heard that Jack's restaurant featured natural plants, indoors waterfalls, and bamboo walls. Behind the restaurant Jack had created a beautiful jungle. Walkways led to exotic spots that featured ponds, beautiful swans floating in the still water, huge arrays of flowers, waterfalls and ornate bridges that adorned the landscaping. It was quite an attraction and people who came to dine also had the privilege of walking through the jungle.

Ralph called him to see if he still had his chimp and was pleased to find out he did. He asked if he would allow them to shoot some photos of Jerry and Judy in exchange for some added publicity for his restaurant, and he readily agreed.

It was a hot summer day when Frank and Ralph arrived with Judy. Their photographer was hoping to get some sensational shots of them in the jungle setting. Just beyond the jungle was a vast field of grown palm trees that Jack sold commercially.

Jack finally met them in the jungle area and told them about the life he and his wife had with Jerry. Jerry was bathed in the bathtub and ate breakfast, lunch, and dinner with them each day. They had taught him to use knives, forks, and spoons. He wore a bib and sat at the table politely with the family as well as with guests. Jack said Jerry was 14 years old and weighed about 100 pounds.

It was good to hear that their training was working. They loved him like a son and essentially brought him up as one.

Around the corner came Mae, holding hands with a rather large chimpanzee walking upright and wearing blue jeans, a Western shirt, and tennis shoes which had a hole cut out to allow room for the big toe.

Wow! thought Ralph. That is one large chimp. Not as big as Hugo but big. Mae was a small, frail woman, not much bigger than Jerry.

Introductions were made all around - including Jerry, who shook hands as well as any gentleman. He immediately took a liking to Judy.

Mae took Jerry's hand and together they walked ahead of Ralph's group, deeper into the jungle area. Judy seemed unimpressed with Jerry. She pulled her hand away when he tried to hold it.

The photographer did a quick exploration and picked a quiet place in a small clearing where a tree stump formed into a bench. Huge leafy plants and a moss-laden waterfall surrounded it. This was where they would take the first series of pictures. Jack sat Judy down with Jerry for the photographer to get his lighting while Mae excused herself to take care of restaurant business.

It was then it occurred to Ralph that maybe Jerry had probably never seen another chimp before.

"Jack, isn't Jerry showing Judy a bit too much affection, kissing her arm, nuzzling up close, and being overly touchy feely with her?"

Jack laughed. "Well, this is his first time meeting another chimp and a female chimp at that. He's just being friendly." Then a sharp, "Jerry, cut it out!" voiced from Jack was all that was necessary for Jerry to stop his playing and mind his manners.

Judy was enjoying every minute of the attention as makeup was applied and hair combed on both chimps by the photographer.

After a few shots, he asked that Jack change Jerry's position.

Jack stood Jerry up next to Judy and put his arm around Judy's shoulder. A few shots were taken and Jerry was back snuggling up close to Judy again.

"Give her a kiss, Jerry. Go on," said Jack, egging Jerry on.

Ralph was getting a little concerned about Jerry's affection towards Judy. Under other circumstances, chimp kissing seems to be universal - all chimps do it, so he didn't think there was any harm in it - except of course, that Jerry was feeling quite amorous and Judy was a female.

Jerry smacked a kiss on Judy's cheek which she didn't like at all and pushed Jerry away. He let out a grunt of discontentment. In the wild chimpanzee world, female chimps do not refuse the affection of a big dominant male chimp, especially one that had never been around another female chimp ever in his life. The photographer was ecstatic.

"That was great," he exclaimed.

But not two minutes went by before Jerry was all over Judy and wouldn't leave her alone.

"Let's take a break for a while so I can load the cameras and find a better angle," said the photographer.

They all relaxed for a moment, talking about which shots would sell the article. The photographer had just finished loading the camera and was setting up his next shot when they heard Judy let out the equivalent of a human scream.

Jack broke a branch off a nearby tree and ran yelling toward Jerry. "Jerry, you bad boy! What are you doing?"

As Jack advanced with the club held high over his head, Jerry changed from a sweet, cuddlesome chimp to King Kong. He rose up on his hind legs, his hair bristling, eyes glowing, and with a primal scream, dropped to all fours and charged Jack.

Startled, Jack fell backward in his effort to get away. Jerry roared at him and then, before Judy could leave, went back and cuddled up to her, sweet as could be, as though nothing had happened.

Things now had gotten out of hand.

Judy was shaking and Ralph could see she was scared. She held out her hand to Ralph as though to say 'get me out of here.'

Ralph started toward her. Jerry stood up and directed his wrath toward Ralph, one hand still holding Judy as he pounded the tree trunk with his fist, hooted his anger and possessiveness, revealing his dagger-like fangs.

Jack was completely in shock. Never had he ever seen anything remotely resembling this kind of behavior from Jerry before. Something had to be done - like now! Ralph took the initiative.

"Jack, have one of your staff go and get all the goodies he can carry from the restaurant - now!"

"What?" Jack yelled in surprise.

"Just do it! Have him bring everything Jerry likes."

Nearby, parked as an attraction, was an old original circus wagon from the days when the circus would travel cross-country, visiting little towns on the way. It had wooden wheels and a row of iron bars that held whatever the circus was presenting that year. Could have been a lion, or monkeys but more likely a "Wild Man of Borneo" sporting a long beard. With wild hair and half naked, he'd lunge at the bars, scaring the people - especially the little ones to tears. After hours, a sharp eye would see him as a roustabout, working around the circus grounds.

The staff fellow was on his way back from the restaurant loaded down with every imaginable pastry and fruit he could carry. The wagon wasn't very big and Ralph, Frank and, with the help of some men standing by, succeeded in pushing it up close to where Jerry was having his day.

"Frank!" yelled Ralph, "Climb up on top and pull the sliding steel door all the way up!"

When done, Ralph got a thick branch from the undergrowth and wedged it in the doorway to prevent it from sliding down. By then, Jerry, still angry, was stomping his feet and hooting as loud as he could. Not for a second had he let go of Judy's arm. She sat frightened, still shaking and scared. Jerry had just gone back to his adoration of Judy when the food arrived.

"Dump everything into the cage - way in the back," Ralph ordered, fishing for things that made sense. The only thing Ralph could think of to entice Jerry away from Judy was food.

Meanwhile, Jerry was all over Judy, touching, feeling, and being intimate. Poor Judy was a basket case. She was afraid of this 'ape' and wondered why Ralph didn't take her away.

Ralph was getting quite worried. Jerry was totally out of control. His first concern was for Judy. Jerry could give her a severe bite to make her submit to his wishes. He was now a danger to the people in the area, and finally to Jack and himself.

They were the main antagonists, he thought. A bite, let alone a full out attack, could rip them apart.

Ralph spoke to Judy as though she was human. She was used to that and even though she didn't understand the words, she understood the inflections.

"Listen, Judy, take Jerry's hand."

He spoke quietly so as not to have her hear the panic in his voice. She understood what Ralph wanted. He had asked that same thing many times when a friend would come up and he would introduce them to her. He would say "take his hand" or 'shake his hand." But in this case it was different. There was no way she wanted anything to do with this "animal."

"Judy, it's o.k. Jerry is not going to hurt you," he lied.

Judy was in shock. Her mind was in a whirl. On one hand, she hated this creature next to her. On the other hand, Ralph, her friend whom she trusted, wanted her to do what she didn't want to do.

"Judy? Go ahead, girl. Take his hand."

Judy looked up at Ralph with a plea for help. Then slowly reached over and did what he said. Jerry was ecstatic. He took it as a sign of submission.

Ralph continued, making her listen to the sound of his voice. "Judy, listen to me. Take Jerry over to the food. The food, Judy."

Ralph emphasized the word food. This Judy knew very well. He could see her trying to comprehend what he was saying. She nodded in an unsure way.

"I want you to take his hand and get up and go to the food."

Ralph could see her take a deep breath, and slowly get up and start to walk.

"Good girl, Judy."

She knew, thought Ralph, she knew. God, what a great animal. Ralph calmly motioned to Frank.

"Get up on the roof of the wagon. Take out the branch. When I tell you, you let that door down as fast as you can. Got it?"

Frank nodded and not to alert Jerry, headed for the wagon slowly.

"When you're up there, lie flat so he can't see you," added Ralph.

Ralph's plan was to get Jerry into the cage with Judy and while he was eating, she could sneak out and close the door. Down deep, Ralph didn't think it would work. Jerry was too smart for that but what else could he do? Time was of the essence. He had to try something.

Due to Jerry's desire for Judy, he walked with her. Under these circumstances he would walk anywhere with her. Ralph realized that although this sexual craving of Jerry's was a primitive urge, neither chimp had ever mated before. It was their basic instinct that was driving them both. Jerry, being the aggressor, was far more anxious. Judy, as the victim, was far less interested.

They were lucky. Jerry was cooperating. Both were headed toward the wagon, that is until a stranger who thought he was some macho animal god walked straight up to Jerry saying things like, "Hey, man, let her go."

In two steps, Jerry charged the idiot, knocking him to the ground. He was back with Judy before she could make a run for it. The man scampered across the ground until he could regain his footing, and then raced away, never knowing how lucky he was. He could have been severely bitten or worse.

By this time, spectators had gathered. Not knowing the danger, they were pressing closer and closer. Ralph yelled to Jack to get those people back. He called some of the waiters from the restaurant to herd them away. Amazingly, the audience was reluctant to go.

Ralph turned his attention back to Judy. "Judy, keep walking, just keep walking. Good girl."

Jerry was being so very gentle with her and was walking alongside her without any problem. As they neared the cage, he stopped and held her back.

"Talk to him, Judy, coax him in. You can do it." This was human talk, not to be understood by Judy but Ralph knew Judy so well his enthusiasm showed in his delivery.

Judy was great. She pulled Jerry's hand as she started to climb into the wagon where all the food was. Jerry didn't even hesitate. He followed her right in.

"Now, sit Judy, sit," he said, hoping she would sit near the door.

Judy did as Ralph said. She sat perhaps five feet from the door. Jerry sat next to her but Ralph could see that he wanted some of that food and that was all the way in back of the wagon. To get some he would have to let go of Judy's hand.

Ice cream, bananas, apples, oranges, cookies; all the things he loved. Fortunately, he hadn't eaten lunch before they came and was starved. A trickle of ice cream ran down the floor of the cage, straight to Jerry. He reached his foot over and rubbed it in the ice cream, then licked it off his big toe. The food had taken his mind off Judy for a while, but he remembered her as he stood up and started to pull and drag her toward the food.

"No, Judy. Stop!"

She knew that stop meant to stop whatever she was doing at the moment. She reached up and grabbed one of the bars on the cage. Jerry put a lot of his strength into pulling but Judy held fast. The floor was made of sheet metal and made it difficult for Jerry to pull without sliding.

"Good girl," Ralph said, gently. "Good girl."

Jerry's sexual attitude was far from gone. However, his hunger pangs had only exacerbated the situation. He reached as far as he could while holding Judy's hand but couldn't reach the food.

The food was becoming an insatiable desire. Finally, not being able to resist, he let go of Judy's hand, raced to the ice cream, smeared his hand in it, and then raced back to Judy.

Holding her hand, he licked the ice cream from his other hand. Ralph had noticed Judy looking at the open door and was pleased she didn't try to make a run for it. She wouldn't have made it.

Ralph knew Jerry would try again. He knew she would never make it out the door until he settled down with the food, and that if Judy tried and failed, she wouldn't have a second chance.

By now, Jerry was drooling for more ice cream and food. He'd let go of her hand but sat there as though testing her. She sat there courageously and baby-talked him. She looked at the open door again.

"No, Judy, no." Ralph could see her wanting to run but she listened and was keeping her cool.

For a half hour, they sat there, sometimes holding hands sometimes not. At least the presence of food had put some of his desire for Judy on hold. Jack's people had done a good job. The goodies were very enticing. Ralph called to Frank whose arms were about to give out. The door was steel and heavy.

"Don't answer me because Jerry will hear you," Ralph said. "But stay ready when I say 'now,' let the door fall."

He nodded his okay.

Ralph was concerned about Judy being hit by the door. He knew Frank was aware also and would have to judge his move. Ralph could see Jerry weighing his odds. He let go of Judy's hand, then slowly moved toward the food.

Ralph said calmly, even though he wasn't, "Judy, stay, stay where you are."

Jerry looked at Judy and then at the food, and then continued moving until he was sitting in the middle of all the food. He started to eat fast, shoving the cake, cookies, and ice cream into his mouth and grabbing all he could with his hind feet and both hands. Ralph saw what he was going to do. He was going to carry it back to Judy.

Now was the time. It would never get any better.

Jerry had a piece of cake smashed in his face, apples in his hand, and a box of cookies held in his feet.

"Judy, come, come, come!" Ralph yelled. "Now, Judy! Come! Go! Go! Go!"

She literally fell out the door.

"Now! Now! Close that f***ing door!" he yelled to Frank.

Frank let the door go. It started to slide, and then got hung up on the sliding trough. Jerry, seeing what was happening, dropped the food and headed for the door.

"Pull, man, pull!" Ralph screamed, desperate.

Frank, using all his strength, pulled again. The door straightened and the steel door came sliding down within a few inches of closing. The wagon was old and the doorframe was out of adjustment.

Screaming with rage, Jerry slipped his hands under the door and, pulling with all his might, started to raise the door. Ralph knew if he got out now he would wreak fury on whoever was within reach.

Ralph raced to the cage, climbed up the steel bars, and threw himself on top of the door alongside Frank until Jerry finally let go and the door slammed shut with a loud thump.

Jerry went crazy. He went into a fury. Screaming like a banshee, he grabbed the bars and threw his full weight against them until he rocked the cage. Ralph saw that the wheels were coming off the ground. Some of the people watching hurried over and stopped the wagon from tipping over. Jerry was rushing back and forth trying to topple the cage. He would have done it, too, if they hadn't held on; it took five men to hold the cage.

He screamed, bounced back and forth, pounded his fists, and thumped his feet. He jumped into the middle of the food pile, throwing it everywhere while slipping and sliding, screaming all the time.

After the cage was tightly secured and Jerry had settled down, his attention now back on the food at hand, Ralph rushed over to Judy who scampered up into his arms. She was a bit bruised and shaken but otherwise all right.

They hugged and hugged, tears slid down Ralph's cheeks. But he managed a smile. Judy gave him her geek look. What a great chimp she was.

The photographer had gotten a few good shots before all hell had broken loose. He felt he had enough for a newspaper spread, so the day wasn't a total waste.

Jack couldn't stop apologizing. He had never, ever seen Jerry do that before. Nothing even close.

"He was like our son," lamented Jack.

"Good thing it wasn't your wife," Ralph replied.

The next day Ralph got a call from Jack. He was crying. "What's wrong, Jack?"

"Jerry's dead."

"What?"

"Dead. I shot him."

"You what?" He couldn't believe what he was hearing.

"I couldn't help thinking about what you had said. You know, about my wife. You were right, it could have been Mae."

The sobbing continued as he reminisced. "He and I used to go out to the palm trees. You know the ones out back?"

"Yeah, I saw them."

Jack could barely speak. "Well, he would push the wheelbarrow and then help me dig the dirt around one of the palms and haul the palm back. He was a good worker."

"Jack. I…" Ralph didn't know what to say.

"Well, I let him dig a hole and I. . . shot…him. Buried him right there." His sobbing was unbearable. "I'll miss him."

Ralph knew it was never easy to end an animal's life. Whether it was the correct decision or not, was not his place to say. Jack had made that decision and he was willing to live with the consequences; life without his friend.

Ralph felt for him and, in some ways, he too, felt responsible for Jerry's death. Had he not come with Judy, the problem would never have happened.

But then again, it would have happened just at another time. And maybe the end result wouldn't have been so good. One cannot raise a full grown chimpanzee in a house and not suffer the consequences. Sooner or later, be it from jealousy, sexuality, psychological makeup, whatever, it will come and when it does, be prepared for an emotional and terrifying experience.

The experience with Jerry added much to Ralph's appreciation of the power and focus of the nature of animals. He was sorry Jerry had to lose his life. That day, he had turned dangerous for all of them, even the patrons at the restaurant who could have been hurt or injured had he become even more ferocious.

Jerry helped Ralph to recognize even more that every creature on this planet had its instincts and to coexist with them, there must be acknowledgement and respect.

Chapter 14

It was an unusually cold day in April. By now, the weather should have turned warm, awaiting the splendor of spring. But as usual, since climate change, one never knew what to expect.

Ralph had arrived back at the ranch after a long meeting with the studio heads about upcoming episodes of Daktari. He was anxious to return as Judy had been showing signs of a cold coming on and he had asked Frank to watch over her in his absence. He walked over to the guys' house expecting Frank to be there with Judy. There was no sign of Judy, but Frank was coming up from the stables where he had gone to check on a mischievously escaped zebra that had to be rounded up.

"Where's Judy?" Ralph asked Frank.

"She's not here?" said Frank, surprised. "I had Linda watching her while I tended to our little escape artist. She should be here," he said, looking around.

They went up to the main house and Ralph found a note on the door saying that Linda had taken Judy to the vet in town.

"That's not like her to just leave and not say anything to me," Frank said. "I'm sorry, Ralph. Let me find out what happened."

Now Ralph was feeling a little anxious. Linda was one of the newer staff members who was dedicated to the animals, but still, experience meant everything when working with exotics. Not only was Judy an important animal in terms of Daktari, her health was the most important part of her care. If something had happened while he was away, he would never forgive himself.

"Don't worry about it," Ralph said, as he ran to his car. "I'll go to the vet myself and check it out."

He was barreling down the dirt drive and out onto the main road before Frank could even answer him.

As Ralph pulled into the vet's parking lot and exited the car, he heard the screaming of a chimp from inside the clinic. It was Judy. He started racing toward the racket. Something was terribly wrong. She was either being attacked or severely hurt. Unbeknownst to Ralph, Judy had turned quite sick in his absence. Linda became worried and, bundling her up, took her to the hospital.

She remembered hearing Ralph talk about his favorite vet, Dr. Andrews, and asked for him when she arrived at the clinic. A man opened a door and emerged into the waiting area.

"Hi, you're Dr. Andrews?" she asked.

Without answering he asked, "What's the problem?"

"My friend here has a small cold but recently it has turned worse, so here we are," she said.

Judy peeked out of the blanket and the vet could see she was quite ill. Her eyes were half-closed and she was shivering.

"How do you know?" he asked with flippant arrogance.

"That she needs treatment? You can look at her and tell."

"Didn't you take her temperature?"

"No. She's sneezing and won't eat."

"Hmm. Really?"

This was one arrogant man, she thought. Bad attitude. He was not one of us. Everybody at the ranch were nice animal loving people. This man was hostile. But she needed Judy to be treated and there was no one else. He never said he wasn't Dr. Andrews so she assumed he was.

"Well, take him over to that big cage over there."

Linda did as she was told. The doctor took out a small bottle of strep/pen and filled a syringe with two cc's of the drug.

"O.K., young lady, put him in that cage."

"She's a girl."

"Whatever, just put her in."

In her mind, she was surprised that Ralph had spoken so well about Andrews. She thought him to be an asshole. The doctor put the needle and syringe in his pocket then closed the cage door. Holding Judy arm's outside of the cage, he flipped a switch. One whole side of the barred cage started to move toward Judy. At first, she didn't seem to mind but as the row of bars came closer, she started to panic. Putting her feet against the advancing bars, she pushed with all her might. But the bars kept coming.

Linda watched as the bars pressed against Judy. She screamed for help but by then the bars held her. She hadn't been this scared since her mother was killed. She defecated and peed struggling to get out. When the bars stopped, she was held tight against the side of the cage.

"What are you doing? That's horrible!" Linda was in tears.

The doctor took the needle out of his pocket and with her arm extended outside the cage, he applied a tourniquet which caused a large vein to show itself. Then slowly he stuck the needle into the vein.

Judy went berserk. She screamed at the top of her lungs. She bit the steel bars. But could not dislodge her arm.

Linda screamed, "Let her go!"

"Can't do that. Now, just a minute more."

The doctor pushed the plunger in as the liquid flowed into Judy's bloodstream. When he pulled out the needle, a long line of blood squirted on his white lab coat.

"Ah! That should do it."

Linda was angry now. "That's horrible. How could you?"

"Better that she die?" he asked.

Linda was horrified. She had never seen anything like this before.

Just then, the door burst open. Ralph, seeing what was happening, ran to the cage and shoved the doctor aside almost knocking him down.

"You crazy bastard!" he yelled.

He pulled the switch and released the bars holding Judy. She was exhausted from trying to escape. Ralph opened the door and she jumped into his arms screaming all the time. Her eyes bulged wide. Poop was everywhere. She was wheezing trying to catch her breath. The doctor was casually taking off his blood stained jacket. Ralph was furious.

"Who in the hell gave you permission to do that? I could have your license. Where is Dr. Andrews?"

Linda looked at Ralph in shock. "You mean, he isn't . . ."

"No, who are you?" Ralph demanded.

"My name is Dr. Aston."

"Well, don't you know, Doctor Aston that there are other ways to subdue an animal. You have probably eradicated some of the most important behaviors I had put into her."

"Like what?"

"Trust for one, loyalty for another."

Ralph could tell the doctor was not listening. He seemed like he couldn't care less.

"It's my oath and duty as a doctor to think of the welfare of the animal above all else. I probably saved her life," he said quite nonchalantly. "Your trust and loyalty would have meant nothing if she died."

Linda was so frightened she was shaking. "Mr. Helfer, I'm so sorry. I didn't know. I thought . . ."

"It's o.k., let's go home. I'll speak to Dr. Andrews directly about this in the morning."

When they returned to the ranch, Linda ran a mild hot bath for Judy and she and Ralph together slowly lowered her into it. She loved to feel the hot water and playing with her rubber ducky. They washed the poop off her and cleaned her. By the end of the bath, she had calmed down and was ready for bed. Ralph was rubbing her down when she pointed to the sore that the needle had left and made her small 'ooh! ooh!' sound.

"Yeah, I know I know, it's a boo boo."

Ralph pulled a small bed close to his. They tucked her in. Judy did her 'life is good' noise as Linda rubbed some body oil on her. Within minutes, she had dropped into a deep sound sleep.

Linda said her goodnight, still apologizing and accepting the responsibility for what happened. "Mr. Helfer, please forgive me, I didn't know, I swear . . ."

"Linda, it's all right," he said putting his hand on her shoulder. "I don't blame you at all. And, please, call me Ralph. We're not formal around here at all."

She nodded her head gratefully, smiled ruefully and left him with Judy. "Goodnight, then, Ralph."

"Night."

He watched her go for a moment and then climbed into bed but couldn't sleep. Did he do wrong? Why was that the procedure? Did that jerk of a doctor do the right thing? Had he been there, he would have called Andrews immediately to see if there was an alternative to the doctor's abrasive behavior. Surely there was another way. Sleep came over him as he felt for Judy's hand lying in the bed alongside of him.

"Sorry, girl."

Normally in the early morning, Ralph would bring hot tea or cocoa to Judy and later sit out on the training building veranda to have breakfast. If it was warm, they would go for a walk. If cold, they took the car. But with Judy still sniffling, her nose running, and showing a low fever, he decided to bring the breakfast to her - hot tea, a biscuit, a bowl of hot soup, and a mix of fruit. A quick sniff and she turned her back on most of it except the fruit and tea. A strange mixture but who's to question the instincts of animals, he thought.

Ralph called Dr. Andrews and told him of the fiasco that had occurred the previous day. Andrews said to bring Judy in so he could give her a thorough examination. He assured Ralph Dr. Aston would be nowhere near the examination room.

Dr. Andrews was an exceptional veterinarian who had specialized in the study of primates. He had been the ranch's vet for years and was a good friend of Ralph's. A warm handshake, a pat on the head for Judy and the doctor and Ralph started on a long line of catching up.

"What's with this doctor of yours? He's quite a handful. I wanted to punch his lights out right then," said Ralph.

"So sorry about all that. He was taught at a school in Germany that when treating an animal, nothing matters except its healing."

"No matter what he has to do to get there?"

"'Fraid so. He must have felt that she had the highly dangerous flu and time was of the essence. Many human doctors do the same. Horrible bedside manners, you know, emotionally down the drain. They don't care and won't even listen to anything that alters their direction. His knowledge is good and he's an expert, but unfortunately, he makes a lot of enemies."

"Why is he here?"

"No choice. I need a backup vet." When I'm busy and can't make my schedule, I have to depend on him. I'll talk to him. He's good, but well, not as nice as I am," he said smiling.

"Well, I think he should go back to school and learn how to be sociable."

"You're right, and believe me, I will talk to him today about the situation. We can't afford to get any sort of bad rep within the animal world. I want this clinic, and I know you agree, to be first rate and respected. So, shall we go check out our friend?"

They headed back to the lab so the doctor could give Judy a full examination. Judy wasn't at all troubled when the doc asked her to open her month, when he put the stethoscope on her chest and inserted an anal thermometer. A box of her favorite candy sure helped. It wasn't long before the doctor gave his diagnosis.

"It's not a cold. She has the flu and I might say one of the bad ones. I'll need to take some more tests."

"Doc," said Ralph sheepishly, "I know a lot about many animal diseases and am constantly learning more, but nuances between the flu and a cold are absent in my knowledge field. What is the specific difference?"

"It's much like us humans, Ralph. A common cold usually comes and goes within a week, typically infecting the upper respiratory system. The flu can hang on for a few months and be more dangerous. It can be lethal to apes as it can infect cells deep in the lungs, causing pneumonia and, in severe cases, death. In fact, we've just received a report that a very strong virus is going around, killer type. It was restricted to humans up until about a month ago. It's a very potent strain."

"So how do we help poor Judy?"

"The best thing is a good dose of strep/pen. It's a mixture of some of the strongest antibiotics one can take."

"How is it administered?"

"By injection. I understand Dr. Aston was successful in giving her a shot of it. I realize his method may have seemed harsh, but he probably saved her life," said Andrews.

"His arrogance is felt by the animals, you know. I bet they can tell he doesn't care about them at all."

"I know, it's just his way. He is so into his work he really doesn't care if he hurts someone's feelings. I promise to speak to him about it."

"Aren't some of his methods a bit outdated? There're new procedures being tried that consider the animal's feelings. And with better results."

"Perhaps. Look, there's no doubt he is truly an eccentric person. He is a good doctor but always wants to do things his way. What he did was wrong. He should have first gotten permission from you but I am sure his thinking was to save the chimp no matter what the cost."

"I would think that all the exertions, fighting that . . . that 'squeeze machine' would take away the strength to fight a disease."

"Maybe, but the bottom line is, Judy seems to have benefitted from Dr. Aston's actions. She is doing fine."

"Doc, seriously, what would you have done?"

"Me? The first thing? Give her a sleeping pill."

On the way home, Ralph was thinking about the future. What if Judy got sick again and had to be given a number of shots. Sometimes the needles have to stay in for a long time. After what happened, he didn't think Judy would ever allow anyone to give her a shot. He thought about it for some time.

By the time he reached home, he had made his decision. I'm going to try, he thought, to not accept a squeeze cage when she gets a shot. I owe it to her. Who knows, someday it could save her life.

Ralph couldn't stop thinking what would have happened had Judy not gone into the squeeze cage. His thoughts ran the gamut of his emotions. She could have died. What would he have told Charlie and what would

Charlie have told the Mathers? That he chose wrong? That he was the wrong person to take care of Judy? Well, it was over and the ordeal had left Judy afraid of squeeze cages and needles. However, on the good side, the shot may well have saved her life.

He wondered if he could get Judy to accept a needle on her own. Nah, impossible. Not after that nightmare. But he was, after all, a behaviorist and it was worth a try. Maybe he should at least give it a chance. He had to come up with a way to make her feel that the shot was enjoyable. Ha. He thought, that should be fun.

He waited a week until Judy was back to her old self. He felt the best way was to do it on a very casual basis. Then on a Monday morning, he began.

First, he placed a bowl of goodies on the table as an incentive. Whenever she showed advancement, a goodie would be offered.

He laid out a bunch of small toys. Perhaps fifteen. They were a mixture of teddy bears, soldiers, balls, and a plastic toy syringe from a toy doctor kit. He jumbled them all together and placed them on a table. Then he brought Judy in. He'd feed her cookies, a Coke, and begin to play with her on the table where the toys were.

He started to toss them to her; she would pick them up and throw them back. Ralph returned the toss. It landed close to Judy. When she saw it, she made a "woof" sound and hit it with the back of her hand knocking it off the table.

Ralph continued to play and nonchalantly picked up the syringe and placed it back in the toys. This went on for some time until Judy finally picked it up and smelled it. Seeing it was a rubber toy, she bit it a few times then returned it to the pile.

Ralph was quite happy with the first day's program. Now for the next step.

The following day they played catch with the syringe. By now, Judy accepted it as just a toy. Ralph waited a few days before proceeding with one of the most important steps.

He replaced the toy syringe with a real one. The new one was made of a clear plastic-type material instead of glass. He placed it on the table among the other objects and continued doing mundane things waiting for her to react to it.

Eventually she saw it. Smelled it, flicked it with her finger a few times to be sure it wasn't alive. Then she picked it up! Fantastic!

The next morning, he put a small amount of harmless saline solution in it. He procured the smallest needle from his own emergency medical supplies. It was so small, it resembled an acupuncture needle, and one could hardly feel it when inserted into the skin. He brought Judy in and let her play.

After a while, he took the syringe, needle, and saline bottle out and placed them on the table. Judy stopped playing and watched from afar what Ralph was doing. As he drew a small amount of liquid from the bottle into the syringe, she got interested and came to watch. As they approached, he turned his back on them so they could not see what he was doing.

It was a method he had used before. Tease to build her curiosity. As she tried to look, he pricked his skin and giggled. Judy was familiar with his laugh. When she tried to peer over his shoulder, he hunched up and made it near impossible for her to see.

Getting more exasperated from the teasing, Judy reached up and with a tug, tried to pull Ralph's shoulder down. But Ralph held firm. Then Judy stood up and rested her head on his shoulder. This time Ralph relaxed his shoulder and let her see. He took the needle and pricked his skin. Then giggled. She knew his giggle from when they played together. So to hear him giggle she knew whatever he was doing was fun. He finally relaxed his shoulder and let her watch.

It was all a way of getting Judy interested in doing it. She shied away from having the needle prick her skin but she did handle the syringe. It took a few days before she would allow the needle to pierce her skin. She would put her head down on the table within inches from where Ralph was piercing his skin. She finally gave in and allowed Ralph to do it to her. She never felt anything but seeing the needle go into her skin was enough to delight her.

The next step was to inject a minimal amount of saline into her skin. Because having seen the needle go into her skin and feeling nothing, injecting the saline proved to be simple.

Give or take a week, Judy was allowing Ralph to inject the saline into her skin. Once she understood it wouldn't hurt, and in fact, could be fun, she relaxed and actually would sit and enjoy it. Ralph figured she was probably the only primate who, with a little help, could give herself an injection!

When Ralph showed his friend, Dr. Andrews, the methods used to train Judy, he was impressed and immediately thought about how he could incorporate the method into his own practice for other animals. However, since most of his other animals were not as smart as Judy or as conditioned to respond to human interaction to the same depth, most of the attempts were unsuccessful. But when it came to Judy, if it was at all possible, she would never be 'squeezed' again to be given a shot.

Chapter 15

Daktari had been picked up for another season and the crew was ecstatic. The scriptwriters were busy working on new ideas. Most of the crew had left to take their leave while the producers were busy arranging for upcoming shows. The new filming was to take place in one month. Not much time to prepare everything but with the pick-up, the adrenaline was flowing and things were hopping.

One of the producers allowed Ralph to take part in some of the major decisions. He sat in the office with others going through budget, location costs, cast, and everything that they could think of to keep the budget down.

"Let's go to Africa," said one of executives.

"What?"

"Sure. The show takes place in Africa but up to now, we've shot everything in California. Not only that, but it will help our budget. By sending a small crew over with the key actors, we wouldn't incur the union's high cost of filming here."

"Wow, sounds like a big move."

"Nah. Not so. Let's check it out. If the trip helps the budget and we could shoot enough second unit, coupled with some first unit material, we could do it."

A few days later, the same group met.

"Well, where are we? How does it look?"

"Looks good. We can save a pile of money by going for three and a half weeks."

"Where would we shoot?"

"Kenya. The dollar rate to the shilling is good, no unions and we have some contact with production people there."

Ralph spoke up. "We also have received calls from people in Mozambique saying they would help us if we decide to come."

"O.k. It's a go. When would we leave?" asked the producer.

"Next week? Wow. That's a lot to get ready."

"Aren't we forgetting something?"

"What?"

"Judy."

"What about Judy?"

"Judy has become a major player in the production. She's practically in every script. If we don't take her, the scenes won't match when we return to shoot the rest."

"Is there any problem in taking her?" His eyes turned to Ralph.

"I don't think so," Ralph said. "Probably need a health certificate. And a passport."

"What?"

"Just kidding. But I have a friend who can help if need be."

"O.k., let's do it."

The crew consisted of six people: Ralph, the producer, director, cameraman, assistant cameraman, continuity - and Judy. It was tight, but everybody knew their job so things should run smoothly.

The next week was chaotic. Cameras were packed, passports obtained. Most of the crew got vaccinations. Judy, with her help, got a few. Ralph was packing and going through the brief scripts of 'acting' that Judy would be required to do. He wanted to be sure she could do all that was expected of her. She had noticed the anxiety of the people getting ready for the trip.

Ralph called Charlie to come and help get Judy ready for the trip. His status as a top official at the Center helped to get Judy her documents to go and return from Kenya just as Ralph had thought.

Charlie helped Judy pack her favorite bath soap, rubber ducky, comb, brush, a few goodies that wouldn't melt in the African heat, and a full wardrobe: shirts, Levi's, pith helmet, boots, underwear, and her favorite doll. The Wardrobe Department wasn't needed on such a short trip so everybody had to take their own.

Judy and C.J. romped and played all day and, in the evening, were given a special dinner. They didn't understand why. Charlie did. While Ralph was on the phone finalizing plans with the rest of the crew, he sat on the edge of the bed watching the two of them eat and enjoy themselves. He reminisced about when he first met them in Africa.

Life is an amazing adventure, he thought. Not only for him but also for Judy. He tried to think how her life in the forest must have been with her mother; living mostly in the trees, eating berries, nuts, different greens and later on, food from the plantations.

Her encounter with the poachers must have been horrible. Then the attack at the plantation, Steve and Marti, God bless them, the Center, all the things leading up to Daktari and now going back to Africa. Full circle, he thought. What do people say? "Like coals to Newcastle" whatever that meant. Would she feel any different? Probably not.

It was a different part of Africa. Yet, Charlie wondered, the Black people, the jungles, who knew what she may feel or remember. All he knew was that she was truly an incredible animal. How she had adapted to the human world was amazing.

He went with Ralph to the airport the next day to see them off. Regulations required Judy to be caged all the way to London. However, seeing as she was a movie star, the airlines would allow her to ride in the passengers' section from London to Nairobi.

Sure she would, thought Ralph with a grin.

Judy's and Ralph's luggage were loaded with the rest of the crew's, along with the equipment, which was all packed in large containers. In big red words, 'Daktari' was stamped on the top side of each crate. With a final hug to Charlie, Judy was off for her African adventure.

She didn't like being caged. Sure, it was larger than the one from before but she wanted to be out with the crew. It was more fun picking their pockets, wrestling, or just plain being with them. A few had beards or moustaches and Judy would spend what seemed to be hours picking and preening them. She, of course, would trade off by turning her back to them to get her back scratched.

She was put in the cargo section down below with a lot of paraphernalia. Nothing alive. If she could read, she would have seen packages going all over the world - France, Italy, China, and the crates to Africa.

The landing was a bit bumpy, but she knew that soon Ralph would be waiting when they opened the door and sure enough, there he was. Good old Ralph, always reliable. A woman wearing a uniform met them and took them over to the rest of the group. Then everybody was ushered out to another more private plane.

"Sorry to rush you but it's either boarding now or staying overnight at a local hotel and leaving in the morning."

"No, this is fine. We can sleep on the plane."

Ralph took Judy over to the Captain. He felt once the Captain met her, he would allow her to be out of her cage on their way to Nairobi. It worked!

"Just keep her in the cage during take-off," he said.

Her cage was put on board in the passenger section.

"O.k., Judy, in you go. You can come out after take-off."

Judy felt the plane leave the runway. It was a different feeling than when she was in the cargo area. Once in the air, Ralph opened her cage door.

"O.k. Judy, you have your own seat near the window," Ralph said clipping a far too big seat belt around her. He also put her special collar and lead on her, and then wrapped it around his hand so she wouldn't have any ideas of playing in the aisles or raiding the galley if he drifted off to sleep.

Judy was glued to the window looking out at the night sky with all of its stars. She couldn't sit still when the moon came into view. What was in her mind? How could she possibly have even a smattering of knowledge about such things? She had seen the night sky in Africa but this was different. There were more stars and they seemed closer. What were they? She wanted to play with them like her marble set at home. She finally sat still watching the sky. She was in deep thought, the wonder showing in her eyes. Ralph pondered if other chimps and their children's children would ever attain the knowledge to understand such things. He could see a reflection of the moon in her eyes. In time, she fell asleep, still sitting in the same position when she was looking out the window, only her eyes were closed. Ralph covered her with the airline's blanket and putting his arm around her, slept.

Everybody in the cabin was asleep when the plane touched down in Nairobi, even Judy. A small truck and a Land Rover were waiting for the group. They piled in wherever there was room. The formality of the office was lost once they landed in Africa. All were the same in stature and rank. No favoritism just equal. Ralph and Judy sat in the back of the truck up against the back of the cab. It was good to be here, thought Ralph. The thrill of being in a country he loved. It was still early morning and he could tell there had been a night of the short rains. Not too wet - just enough to keep things green and beautiful.

They headed up country into the Aberdares, a thick, sometimes impenetrable mountain forest. Animals abounded here. Elephants, rhinos, leopards - all kinds of antelope, including the rare Bongo antelope. They arrived about midday when the weather was the hottest. A small lodge was to be their home away from home for the first week. The hospitality was the very best.

Ralph discovered that the wealthy people in Kenya were just like the wealthy of any country. They could afford to hire help to clean their rooms, make their beds, cook their meals, serve their food, keep their gardens well-tended, drive their cars, wash their clothes - and the list went on and on. Since they were guests, this allowed his crew to concentrate on the business of film making. They were spoiled by the kindness and the generosity of their Kenyan aides and appreciated having time to do their more creative and business activities. He knew he would not have such luxuries once he returned to the United States and the ranch. He would be returning home to chores that here, someone else would do. Sitting out on the veranda, watching the sun go down, drinking a "sundowner," made him yearn to live the rest of his life here.

"How's it going, Ralph?"

It was Marshall Thompson. Marshall was one special person. Always smiling, ready to pitch in and do whatever was necessary. He sat down and long after the sun had gone behind the mountains and after a few sundowners, they spoke of many things. They were both of the same mind. Lovers of nature, animals, and the tribes. Especially the Masai, Samburu, Turkana. They were the ones who seemed to hold on to their traditions. But there were forty-five other tribes here in Kenya alone.

Sleep came easily that first night. It had been a long day. After a hearty breakfast, off they went to find the best place to do their shooting. Judy was feeling her oats, jumping around, messing up people's hair, running off with the coffee pot. The shooting that was needed was mainly fillers - shots that were to be used in-between the shooting of principal photography. Many were of Marshall stalking through the forest, walking across the veldt with animals in the background, talking with African tribesmen. They filmed lions on a kill, lions chasing game, cheetahs with babies, herds of elephants, monkeys in the trees. These shots would be integrated into film that had either already been shot or would be upon their return.

When they were finished with the shots in and around the lodge's acreage, they moved deeper into the African environment, and their accommodations became more primitive, living in tents rather than rooms with help. It was Kenya at its most beautiful – raw and native. The sun was brighter, the air crisper, the night skies overcrowded with shimmering stars. It wasn't a movie set with a commissary around the corner or trailers for the actors; this was where the Daktari of the imagination actually existed.

Ralph and the crew found new dedication to what they were doing, in order to bring their understanding of this country to the loyal audiences in the United States and around the world. They were bringing authenticity to those who watched their show about a caring doctor studying and helping the wild animals in Africa.

They had turned in early one night as they had a sunup shot to do. Since Kenya was on the equator, all the days were twelve hours long so the sun came up around 6:30 each morning and set the same time each night.

It was in the middle of the night that Ralph heard a scream. He grabbed his flashlight and raced out into the darkness. There was nothing worse than running in the dark, tripping on roots, stepping on stones wondering what had happened. Other people were on the move as well, all running in the direction of the cry.

Five flashlights lit up a petrified half-nude woman standing in the dark with her panties hanging around her feet. Fortunately, she was wearing a shorty nightgown. She was crying hysterically. It was Jane, the continuity woman. She had ventured in the dark to go potty. The potty tents were small, four by four square tents with a potty in the middle. They were called "long drops" as they were freshly dug each time the crew moved to another location.

She had found it all right with the help of her flashlight. Once seated, she noticed a rather large boulder that was protruding into the tent. Quite massive it was, as high as her head while sitting down. She realized she hadn't noticed it before but then remembered there were a few 'long drops' so it may have been another one. As she stood up to take care of her toiletry, she laid her jacket on the boulder.

And the boulder moved!

Then it gained height.

It was a full grown hippo!

As it stood up and proceeded to turn around to find out what had caused something to interrupt its sleep, it took the whole tent with it. Jane ran through the zippered door, getting tangled in its canvas, screaming her head off - which prompted the hippo to panic. He let out a bellow and raced toward the river, dragging some of the tent with him.

It took four sundowners and a lot of coffee before Jane stopped shaking. The askari (security guard) had fallen asleep and didn't hear her getting up.

The next day Jane had to put up with the entire crew teasing her about the big time she had last night. She was a good sport about it.

The sounds of the jungle at night caused Judy to be a bit restless. She didn't sleep well for the first few nights, perhaps due to her experiences but as time went on, she was getting used to it and would finally fall asleep.

There was one shot that was needed where Judy, in a playful mood, climbed a tree and when Marshall walked under it she launches herself onto him.

While the camera crew was setting up their equipment, Ralph took her over to the tree. With a wave of his hand, he said, "O.k. Up you go." She looked at the tree and started to whine. "Go ahead, girl, up you go."

With this, he gave her a boost. She screamed, jumped from his arms, and took off running.

"What in the world? What was all that about?"

She came back from her run quite shaken up and refused to go up the tree. Ralph tried everything to coax her to go up but when he saw her shaking, he realized that there was something in her past that he was not privy to. Something so scary that even climbing a tree was an impossible task. He hugged her, spoke to her in a calm voice and gave her some tea.

Then, he had an idea. He got a rather large bush with heavy branches that resembled the ones in the tree and propped it up on a table. They dug a hole alongside of the table. The cameraman put the camera in the hole looking up. The angle on the camera made it appear that you were looking up into a tree. He then put Judy on the branch. In the camera view finder, it looked like she was up in a tree. Then they had Marshall walk by and she leaped onto him from there. Looked o.k.

They filmed different shots for the better part of a week before deciding to pack up and head to Mozambique for the second half of their shoot. Mozambique had just opened a huge animal reserve called Gorongosa. They were told it was the most beautiful part of the country, an untouched virgin area where even the local tribes who lived in there were still primitive. It would give them an even more authentic production.

They were told to be careful, as the animals were still frightened of people and cars and therefore more dangerous. By the same token, it was that wildness that they wanted to shoot. Ralph was anxious to go and Judy was getting a bit rambunctious. He thought she missed C.J.

Before leaving on the trip, Ralph had told Charlie of their itinerary and when he found out they were going to Beira, a city on the coast of Mozambique, he excitedly told Ralph that that was the last place he knew where Steve and Marti were. He asked Ralph if it was at all possible for him to stop by so they could see Judy again. Ralph promised if they had time, he would.

"Surely they must know that Judy's a big star now," he said.

"Yes," said Charlie, "I've written them and told them, even sent some of her publicity photos, but since I never heard back from them, I don't know if they ever received them."

"Well, I'll try for a surprise visit, but can't guarantee it."

Charlie knew that Ralph would keep his promise if he could. It would be a happy reunion, he thought, especially for Marti and Judy.

Chapter 16

They flew into Beira, a port city that exported among other commodities, coconuts and cashews. For the better part of two days, they relaxed on the beach and explored some of the ancient ruins left by the Portuguese. Being on the coast, the city was famous for its seafood, so they scarfed down fresh shrimp and crab at every meal. None of it appealed to Judy. But she made up for it by stuffing herself on mangos and papayas.

Ralph made a trip with Judy to the address Charlie had given him but when they arrived, they were told that the Mathers had moved and left no forwarding address. The old woman who answered the door did a double take as she looked at the man standing there, holding hands with a chimp dressed in jeans and a khaki shirt. Ralph was going to explain but then thought better of it, giving her a polite goodbye, and letting the woman ponder the event all day. Judy blew her a friendly raspberry as they moved down the street.

After filling their supply list, they met José, the pilot, a Portuguese man who claimed he had been flying "deeze jungles for many years, so now, doncha worry none, o.k.?"

No one had said anything about being concerned with his ability to fly the plane - until then. They boarded a twin-engine private plane called a 'flying goose.' It seemed bigger than they needed. They loaded the plane with their equipment; enough to keep them in the jungle for two weeks at a place called the Gorongosa Camp. By now, Judy was seldom in her cage. She was one of the crew. The director gave her a tee shirt with the words 'movie star' on it.

José had purportedly made arrangements with the local natives to clear the brush and fill any potholes on a small dirt runway not far from where the camp was. He was amazed by Judy. He couldn't believe that an animal could be so smart.

"She can be my co-pilot. Come, sit up front with me," he said to Judy.

She had never sat up in the pilot's cockpit and Ralph was afraid she might accidently flip a switch or press a button.

"I don't think that would be wise," he said.

"O.k., so you sit with her," José said, determined to have her up front.

José gave Judy a pilot headset to wear. She could hear the pilot talking to the Beira airfield.

Ralph buckled his seatbelt around her and put his headset on.

"Can she drive a car?" José asked.

"Well, sort of," he replied, smiling.

"Good, then I teach her to fly." He seemed absolutely serious.

"No, I don't think so. It will distract her from doing her acting in the movie."

He accepted that as a logical explanation, for which Ralph was thankful.

With everyone settled in, they took off heading for their jungle destination. The jungle came up quick. Miles and miles of what appeared to be impenetrable, thick jungle. Because Mozambique was on the coast of the Indian Ocean, the temperature was generally hot and the air humid. The plane had no air conditioning and it was stifling inside.

Thirty minutes into the flight they dropped down to skim the treetops, flying lower than Ralph would have thought safe.

"Why so low?" he asked.

"I'm looking for the landing strip."

"You don't know where it is?"

"Not really," said José in a mixture of Portuguese, Aramaic, and English. "I know general area but no runways here. Only they clear patch of the jungle for us to land. Easy. Do all the time in the jungle. I tell them plane size and they cut jungle to fit but, don't worry, I find soon."

They circled an area for ten minutes, nothing.

"Gas getting low. We go back - try tomorrow," José said calmly.

He put the plane in a smooth arc to turn around. By now, the director had come up to the cockpit and said, "Wait a minute. Didn't you fill the gas tank when we left Beira?"

"No. Only half."

"What? You only fill half a tank. Why?"

"Yes, petrol is very expensive. Figured trip would only use half tank. Let next pilot buy his own."

"This isn't your plane?"

"No! No! I rent. Like you."

"Hey, guys, I think I see the spot!" cried the cameraman, now standing behind the director.

José banked the plane and came around over the spot the cameraman had seen.

"Good spotting, Mr. Cameraman. Sí, that is it."

From the air, it looked more like a helicopter landing pad, thought Ralph.

He and the others were still steaming about the half tank but since they had found the landing spot, it was quickly forgotten. At least for now. José did a buzz over to check out the runway.

"The landing strip going to thump!" he yelled. "Better to hang on."

"Hang on to what?" voiced Jane.

Ralph tightened Judy's belt wishing he had left her in the cage. He tightened his arms around her and held her tight. She thought he was showing her affection and gave him a kiss on the cheek.

As they approached, the landing spot grew bigger. The jungle had been chopped on either side of the dirt runway. There were holes and brush still on the strip and as the plane's wheels touched down, Ralph for one was quite happy even with the bumpy landing. Whatever José's failing as a businessman was, he made up for in flying. He was indeed a good pilot.

The six well-built young men who had cut the runway met them. They also served as their luggage bearers. A couple of near-naked boys, perhaps ten years old were their interpreters. They seemed scared of the group and stayed a good distance away yelling to them what the young men would say. They were all afraid of Judy. One man said she should be killed.

"She is a human in an ape's skin."

Actually, Ralph thought the same many times but this was different.

"She is an evil spirit and should be killed."

The plane's motor taking off drowned out whatever else he said. The engines roared as José waved his goodbye. "See you in a couple of weeks!" he yelled. "Adiós – bye, Judy."

Ralph had Judy wave back, but he wasn't sure if it was a good idea. José circled once overhead, dipping his wings, and then disappeared into the clouds. I hope his fuel is enough to get back to Beira, Ralph thought.

The camp was a good hour's walk from where the plane had landed. Judy stayed closed to Ralph, frightened of the jungle and its noises.

Upon arrival at the tent camp, they met Alfonso, a man of Indian/African heritage with a rustic greyish, brownish, blackish beard who owned the camp. He wore a hat that looked like an elephant had sat on it. A dirty old bush shirt showing ample stains of sweat. Camper shorts and boots with no socks made up the rest of his attire.

"Welcome, welcome, my friends. I hope the walk was not too tiring. And you, my lady," he said turning to Jane, "should relax and have a cool drink."

It was obvious immediately that Mr. Alfonso was attracted to her.

"And what have we here?" asked their host attempting to pet Judy's head. "A cute ape?"

She pushed his hand away and gave her geek face.

"Her name is Judy," Ralph said.

"Really, not an ape name." He questioned, "You named her after a human? Hmm? Yes, how strange. Well, let me show you all to your tents."

They had a short dinner of God knows what. It didn't matter - they were all too tired to care. Even Judy fell asleep at the table.

Morning came far too early. A quick shower was in order. Boiling water was produced from a huge pot set on hot coals. A man poured the water into a canvas bag above the shower. A spigot under the bag regulated the flow. By the time the water went through the procedure, it had warmed up a bit to produce an excellent shower. After breakfast they loaded the camera and headed out into the bush. Alfonso was their guide as well.

The jungle was alive with plants Ralph had never seen before. Animals darted across their path occasionally. Alfonso carried a rifle and, after seeing a few elephants and buffalos at close range, it was a reassuring sight.

On their second day, they ran across a small group of villagers. They had been collecting foods from the jungle, their hands and arms were full. Upon seeing the group, they dropped their pickings and ran into the thicket. Some were sobbing, others whimpering.

Judy had been walking with them, standing upright wearing her movie star tee shirt. When they called to them, a few who had been sobbing fell to their knees.

"Alfonso, what in the world are they scared about?" Ralph finally asked, concerned.

He smiled a big grin. "It's your hairy one. They think she is 'Ralph son' - and believe she is the devil."

"Just like at the plane," Ralph said. "Haven't they seen a chimp before?"

"No, only monkeys."

"Please explain to them that she is not the devil."

"They won't listen. Be careful, my friend, most of the tribe here will want to kill her."

"What?"

"Oh yes, her presence here is taboo."

From that time on, Ralph never let her out of his sight.

Within a few days they had gotten most of the footage they needed.

Arriving back at camp they showered, had a sundowner and as the sun set, they headed for the mess tent.

There was an African cloth laid over the food on the table. One could see it was covering a good deal of food. They sat down wondering if they should lift off the cloth. The producer started to lift one end of the cloth.

"Ah! Ah! Not yet." Alfonso had just arrived. For once, he looked clean and well kept. "My good friends, I have prepared a special treat for you. Especially for our dear lady, Jane. Being the only human woman present, I wish to extend my friendship to her and thanks to you all."

With this, he whipped off the cloth to reveal the full body of a wildebeest laid out across the table, horns and all. It was obvious that it was freshly killed. Everything was intact, just cooked and put back in the same place it was originally. The outer and inner body had been cleaned and scrubbed. The horns polished. Inside the cavity lay the cooked meat and organs of those which had been there before.

In the lower extremities lay the testicles that had been cooked and laid on leaves on the same spot they originated from surrounded by various fruit. The stomach and intestines were cooked and laid out in a rather fancy design on a large leaf. The heart was placed in a wooden bowl and laid where it used to live. The head was split open and the cooked brains lay within on a leaf with mango, banana, and coconut placed around it. The meal was undoubtedly a labor of love meant for Jane.

There was a long silence at the table. Judy was the first to indulge. She reached over and grabbed the mango and banana.

"Dig in," said Alfonso.

That did it, Jane, on the verge of up-chucking, ran from the table. They all sat still not knowing what to do. It was truly the most unappetizing display of organs and body parts most had ever seen. It resembled an autopsy in a medical lab. Alfonso noticed the shock his guests were feeling.

"You don't like my dinner? No worry, it's o.k. My staff will eat well tonight."

With a clap of his hands, bowls of tree tomatoes, figs, berries, bananas, pau pau, and mangos were brought in along with bowls of rice, potatoes, and vegetables. The wildebeest was quickly taken away to be enjoyed by those in the know.

"Thank God," murmured a few.

Next morning the group found Alfonso intensely listening to the mobile. Jane went to apologize for her actions last night but he waved her off. There was something in Portuguese coming over the mobile.

Alfonso always had his mobile phone with him. It seemed to be crackling in Portuguese garble most of the time. Ralph couldn't make any sense out of it.

"Alfonso, what are they saying?"

"Many things. Especially where the guerrillas are."

"The what?"

"The guerillas. The rebels. They have been fighting the government for years. We need to watch where they are. They come to villages, rape the women, kill the men, and take the children for workers. They're bad, so very bad."

"We heard before we came about them but that they were far from here."

"It's true but you still have to keep aware."

"So what else is coming over your 'world news' mobile?"

"Not much. Not far from here, some nuns were in a small Volkswagen. One you call 'the bug.' A bull elephant attacked the car, rolled it over a few times, and knelt on it."

"Anyone alive?"

"Yes, all of them. It was a miracle. The rangers just found them. They couldn't get out of the car for two days."

"Your mobile is like our television. We get all the news just like you," said the director.

A slight rain had canceled the day's shooting and it looked like they would be in camp for the rest of the day. They sat around drinking and laughing about the wildebeest dinner, even Alfonso.

"You Americans can swallow raw oysters, eat blood red steak, but our Portuguese meals are too what? Too real? Ah! You miss the best," he added with a smile.

Alfonso's mobile blared again. This time he spoke with the caller. "What? Where? Uh huh. When? Uh huh. O.k. Get hold of José, tell him to get in here fast. Doesn't matter what plane, just have him come."

The group had heard the dialogue.

"What's up, Alfonso?"

"It's not good. The guerillas have moved into our area. They are coming this way."

"What?"

"I told you; you never know about them. They must have been unnoticed until they reappeared in the jungle a few kilometers from here. Perhaps they saw your plane landing."

"A few kilometers? That's like right here. O.k., everybody. Start packing. Now!"

People ran in every direction.

"When is the plane coming?"

"As soon as they can find José."

"Where is he?"

"They don't know. He wasn't planning on coming until Friday. That's two days from now."

"So get another pilot."

"Only he knows where we are."

They heard a shot.

"It's them," said Alfonso. "They've crossed the Lord Albert River."

"Do you think they know where we are?"

"Hard to say."

The next hour found all the crew equipment packed in large canvas bags ready to go. The camp men stood by ready to leave. Time was running out. Everybody was huddled around the mobile waiting for news. The mobile crackled. A voice came on.

"They found José. He was getting a plane but he said the rebels were too close to the landing site. They must know you're here and waiting for you to return to the landing site to fly out. We have to cut a new landing strip."

"Where?"

"Near camp."

"You won't have time to travel."

"This is a very heavy thicket jungle here. That's why they cut the last one where it was."

"Forget that. Cut a new one. Now!"

Just then, another voice cut in. "Hey, my friend. We are coming for dinner." A laugh. "You want to know how close we are?"

Another shot.

"That's close."

The phone went dead.

Alfonso opened one of the bags and pulled out a bunch of machetes. Handing one to each of the group he said, "I'll show you where. Just cut the brush as low as you can."

One of his men came over. "We can't work."

"What?"

"It's that human ape. He did this. We have to kill him or we will all die!"

Ralph grabbed Judy and held the machete Alfonso had just given to him in a menacing position.

"Don't even go there. She is no demon," he said.

Alfonso yelled at his man. Some argued back. It was all in Portuguese so they had no idea what was being said. Then, to their astonishment, two of the men walked off into the bush.

"O.k. Now. Everybody, get to work."

Alfonso showed everybody the place to cut and cut they did. It was hard work. Ralph kept Judy close by, watching that the workers didn't get too close with their machetes.

"Have you heard from José yet?"

"No, I'm getting a bit worried; we have to be out of here by 5:30."

"Why 5:30?"

"Do you remember the Beira airport, where you landed?"

"Yes."

"Do you remember how small it was?"

"So?"

"The Beira airport has no runway lights."

"So?"

"So you can't land at night. They have to be there before the sun goes down."

"Shit. I can't believe all this."

"Let's hope that José makes it in time."

There had been no contact with José for the last hour. The landing strip was a mess but Alfonso felt he could land here. If...

"If? If what?"

"If he brings in a small plane. Let's keep working."

"Never mind. He's here."

"What? Where?"

"I can hear him."

Sure enough the sound of a plane was coming.

Then like an explosion, a plane just missing the trees zoomed overhead.

"It's José!" yelled Alfonso. "It's a small plane, thank goodness. Get ready, everybody."

The next time they heard the plane it was coming in hopefully to land. It seemed to hesitate in midair as it settled down quietly on the strip. It looked like it was going too fast to stop at the end of the clearing. But José, God bless him, pulled it off. He turned the plane and taxied back to the starting point keeping the motor running. They all clamored over him. Jane ran a roll of kisses down his cheek.

"Ok. Ok. Everybody. Look, we have to hurry. The sun is going down and we have to hurry." Equipment, cameras, and packs were thrown in the plane. "Pack them in the front," said José. "People too."

Ralph rushed to Alfonso who stood back from the plane. "Come with us. It's too dangerous here."

"No, you go on. I know the jungles. I'll be o.k."

White people hugged his loyal men for probably the first time in their lives. Judy offered her hand. They hesitated, and then one by one they shook her hand.

"O.k. Everybody. All on board." José whispered to Ralph, "Hope we not too heavy."

They boarded and locked the door. Ralph looked back to wave to Alfonso and his men but they had already disappeared into the bush they knew so well. The plane, much smaller than the first one, found everybody piled together on the floor as well as the seats. The equipment was scattered everywhere.

"Stay up front as best you can," ordered Alfonzo.

Judy was crammed in between Jane, the director, and Ralph. The single motor roared, the plane lurched forward and then, picking up speed, raced down the bumpy dirt path. The end of the runway was coming up fast.

"We're not going to make it, are we, José?"

Ralph looked at his face. It was a sweaty, hard-set, concentrated, determined face. Just at the right moment, he pulled back on the stick and the plane shot up taking a few light branches with it. He circled trying to gain altitude.

"She not coming up." He spoke low so only those close could hear him. "We too heavy. Take out seats. Now!" he ordered.

"WHAT?"

"OUT! OUT!"

The doors were opened and every seat was pulled from its foundation and thrown out the door.

"She coming up but not enough. Look, I head for rift, two thousand feet deep. We clear jungle below."

"So do it!"

"Maybe we not reach Beira before sundown. If we get there after dark, no way to land."

"And if we don't try?"

"We go back."

"To where?"

Silence.

"O.k. Let's go for it."

All heads said to try.

He raced away to the rift. Moments later over the rift, he got the lift he needed, and then made a beeline for Beira. The sun was settling on the edge of the mountain. Ralph knew that once they started to descend, it would be below the horizon and only a bit of light would show.

Then they saw it. The airport. Ralph clenched Judy's hand so hard she winced. But she stayed quiet as though she knew there was something happening of importance.

As they descended, the sun disappeared, the light faded. José was committed. The runway was all but gone. A smidgen of light remained for a split second, and then was gone and so was the runway! He knew he was direct on his approach but he couldn't see it! None of them could.

He had one small light on the front of the craft he had turned on. It was used for airport parking. They knew the runway was in front of them but he couldn't see when the wheel would touch down. Too steep and he would crash, too high and he would go back up into the sky. José practically stood up trying to see the runway. The parking light cast a small beam. It was enough. José, for just that moment, saw the ground and eased the plane on to it.

They were down.

Safe.

"You o.k., Judy?"

She looked at Ralph with her geek face.

"Gimme five."

Chapter 17

The African trip was on everybody's lips. What an amazing experience. It was something out of a novel. Who would have imagined. At first, many of the crew thought they were pulling their leg.

"Not true."

"Impossible."

"You're making it up."

But when they were told all the details: how they had heard the guerillas talking on the shortwave and the firing of the shot and the plane's arrival, they believed. Being back at the ranch after such an adventure almost seemed tame, even in the middle of all the animals around. It was a relief to contend with simply filming again without the fear of guerillas on their heels and airplanes searching for darkened runways!

The equipment had to be completely cleaned. They were lucky that the camera lenses weren't scratched.

"My biggest scare," spoke Ralph, "was when the local bushmen wanted to kill Judy. There is a lot of tribal juju over there. To them Judy was evil and was jinxing the situation."

Ralph made a trip with Judy to the Center to tell Charlie what had happened. Charlie was in awe as Ralph gave him all the awful details.

"They're even talking about doing one of the shows based on what happened."

"Well, it would make a very exciting episode."

"Another thing, Charlie," Ralph said, his voice softening. "I wasn't able to find Steve and Marti. When Judy and I got to the address you gave me, seems they'd moved and left no forwarding address. I didn't know what else to do. Where else to look."

Charlie shrugged. "Don't know what else you could have done. I know Marti would have loved to see Judy again. I don't even know how to get in touch with them. I suppose I could call the ranch and see if Karimi has heard from them. I mean, after all, they didn't desert everyone. It is still their property. But I think Steve was more worried about Marti than the ranch."

"Well, at least it's a start. Let me know what happens."

Judy had lost a bit of weight during her African adventure but nothing to be concerned about. She was fit and took up her place in the series with the rest of the actors.

Within a week, everything returned to normal. The series was going strong and the weather, which was always a concern, kept its distance. Weather and budget were the two adversaries. If it was cloudy, photography became an issue. The big "brutes," giant searchlight-type lights, would need to be hauled out of the warehouse and light the scene to match what had been previously shot.

If it rained, a whole new scene was instituted. Either scenes for the show were shot, which was very difficult, or the rain was incorporated into the existing one. Whichever was chosen, shooting a series or feature needed quick-thinking professionals.

And Daktari had the best. They shot a one hour show every six days. So, you can imagine if something happened that slowed down, let alone stopped the pace, the head office could be heard all the way to the set – some fifty miles away! However, in any business it was always the money. Unfortunately, sometimes it was more important than what was shown on the screen.

During filming, everyone concentrated hard on the tasks at hand. Animals at the ranch and on the set needed caring and grooming, trainers needed to work with them to ensure the specific behaviors necessary so the production would be accomplished correctly and safely.

Everyone needed to be patient with them and Ralph supervised most of the activities himself, along with Frank. Together they made sure the animal performers were ready, on cue, and most importantly, in the mood. There was no way to coax a lion or cheetah into a 'pretend attack' if they were distracted for one reason or another. Directors, producers, human actors, and crew had to be easy-going, all the while watching the clock tick and the money spent.

It was a tricky business, this 'show business' and with animals asked to perform at a precise time, even having to do a 'take two' or 'take three' was extremely tricky – but with exotic animals that are wild – it was even trickier. And after weeks of shooting, everybody was looking forward to the upcoming holiday season.

A week before Christmas the Daktari crew and actors were about to go on leave for a couple of weeks to enjoy the holidays. Before they left, the producers had arranged for a Christmas party to be held in the restaurant on the ranch. The production company had been feeding the crew, trainers, and staff every day which numbered over one hundred fifty people so it would be big enough to hold the crew, actors, and their friends.

Everybody pitched in and turned the restaurant into Santa's house. It glistened with colorful lights, fake snow, and ornaments of all kinds. Some of the staff brought their children and they, in turn, brought many items for the tree.

Ralph didn't want to cut down any live trees, so they built one. A large pine tree had fallen recently and was still quite green. Its branches a bit broken, some brown, some green. The carpenters went to work on it and by adding other branches, tacked here and there, made a tree that standing among other live ones, could carry its own. Getting it in the door was quite a feat but with all participating, they managed.

Ralph felt that because the series was a hit mainly due to the animals, he decided to bring a few of them to the party. He wanted only those that would fit into the group. He chose Judy, Clarence, and Kip, his tiger. They all got along well; however, he had to watch Judy as she was always teasing Clarence by pulling his tail at every chance she got. He brought Modoc but she was limited to being outside as she wouldn't fit through the restaurant door.

"How about Oliver?" suggested one of the trainers.

"He's not part of the Daktari group," voiced another.

"I know but it would be good for him to get out and see how the other half lives."

It was said as a joke but there was meaning behind it. Oliver needed to be involved with other people. So far, he had limited exposure to the trainers who were around him most of the time. True, Ralph had heard from Charlie how the

Sasquatch experience was a huge success, but it only showed Ralph just how great an animal Oliver was.

"He deserves to be here. He's come a long way."

"Well, okay," Ralph said. "Be alert though."

"Great," said the trainers, and off they went to get him.

Ralph put two trainers in charge of each animal. He never knew when something unforeseen may happen and two men had a better chance of controlling the situation. But Ralph didn't kid himself. Lions and tigers had no idea how to have fun at a party. They just enjoyed being with their friends and the guests enjoyed them being there.

Everybody was in good spirits. Some came wearing Santa Claus outfits. Gifts were passed around; toasts were given to the actors as well as a few speeches. Eggnog, hot toddies, with a good dash of rum, was the drink of the evening. Helium balloons were tied everywhere and some floated to the ceiling, with notes in them giving away prizes to the lucky ones who popped them. Some of the wardrobe girls made outfits for the animals. Judy wore her Santa's elf outfit all green and red. Her elf-curved tipped shoes were a delight. Both Clarence and Kip had handmade jackets all brightly made in red and white. The secretary had made small stars that sparkled in Clarence's mane.

Modoc arrived wearing all kinds of Christmas paraphernalia: bells hanging from a decorated Christmas blanket, a merry Christmas note written in washed-off letters across her broad head. Not being able to fit through the restaurant door, she hung her head inside the doorway while people fed her enough goodies to give even an elephant a bad stomach. Popcorn, candy, soda pop, all went the way of Modoc's trunk on the way to her tummy.

Judy was the life of the party. She got right into the fun playing with the crew and eating far too much cake. Some of the crew had bought her a few clothes and she had a ball putting them on.

Oliver arrived looking his aloof self. He walked upright, big and strong wearing a Santa Claus red cone hat. As dignified and respectful as he was, you couldn't help breaking up at his dignified attitude while wearing that silly hat. You could see a glint in his eye whenever something unusual happened - like people dancing, a burst of laugher erupting in the crowd, hearing a joke or maybe Judy coming over to him and planting a big kiss on him.

His biggest thrill of the evening was bursting balloons. One by one, he picked them up, held them in his hands, and then started to squeeze. His eyes squinted in anticipation of what was to come. As the balloon would get close to bursting, the pressure mounted. His mouth dropped open, the tip of his tongue hung out. Pop! It exploded. He did a reserved giggle and picked up another balloon.

The staff had invited a group of children from a local orphanage to join in their party. About thirty-five were bused over and arrived as the party was in full swing. They gave the children their own place adjoining the main building. Dozens of gifts were handed out to them. Modoc gave the kids rides. George, the ranch manager and the one with the biggest belly, became Santa Claus, beard and all. Judy, wearing a beard and hat was Santa's helper and together they handed out gifts for all the children.

At about eleven o'clock, the doorbell rang. Jack, one of the crew members, answered the door to find five rough looking guys all in their late teens standing at the door. They were wearing bandanas around their foreheads, denim jackets and torn jeans. They all had holstered knives in their belts.

"What's up?" asked Jack. Then looking at their attire, he remarked in a joking way, "You have the wrong party. Halloween isn't till next October."

"Hey, asshole, we're here to join the party," said one of the guys who appeared to be the leader.

"Yeah, man, we want to come in," said his cohort.

"Were you invited?" asked Jack, blocking his way.

"Yeah. Sure we were. We're the tribe."

"That's it? That's what you're called?" Jack noticed a few of his buddies had joined him at the door.

"Yeah. You got a problem with that?" Before Jack could answer, the leader started to push his way in. "Doesn't matter. We're here and we're coming in."

"Hey, man!" said another. "We need to sit on Santa's lap and tell him want we want."

At this point, a few of the 'tribesmen' slid their hands back to their knives and undid the holster clips. Jack and his buddies backed off, not quite sure what to do. The tribe pushed their way in and headed for the main room where the party was in full bloom.

One of them went over to the makeup girl and started to hit on her. Another went behind the bar and helped himself to a beer.

The party fun stopped as the tribe infiltrated the restaurant. Trainers and some of the crew all joined in a shoulder-to-shoulder block to keep the guys away from the main party. A couple of the tribe pulled their knives out.

Jack, himself a big guy, stood firm along with his buddies trying to hold the line. "Look now, why don't you all just back on out of here? We don't need or want any trouble."

"Look, big daddy," said the tribe leader, "We're here. Okay? We know we're outnumbered but it don't give no mind. You can bring on all your shaggy ass friends, we don't give a shit. It won't matter. Someone's going to get cut. So back off."

Later, they were to find out the "tribe" as they called themselves were well known by the police. They had been involved in a number of robberies, a few knifings and were related to another group in the selling of drugs.

Before the tribe came in, Ralph had just finished handling Clarence for a few photo shots with some of the guests and still had him on his leash. When the music in the restaurant stopped, Ralph headed over to see what the commotion was about. As Ralph approached, a few of them called out, "Hey, Clarence, how's it hanging?"

Another reached over to touch him. They knew the animals were specially trained.

"If you think we're afraid of the animals, think again. We know they're tame or you couldn't work them on TV with movie stars."

Immediately Ralph could tell they were all either drunk or on drugs. These were always the hardest ones to deal with.

"You have to leave, now," he said.

"Who the f..k are you?" answered the leader.

"Santa Claus. Look. Why don't you take a few beers and go?" He was sweating from the realization that they would start fighting.

"Yeah, we want Santa to give us what we want," said the leader.

His speech was slurred and he was unsteady on his feet. It's true, Clarence was not the animal to put fear in anyone, especially when he was wearing all his Christmas decorations. But there was one who could scare the piss out of most, Kipling, a big tiger they had trained to attack non-aggressively. That is to say, he would snarl, jump on someone, even grab their arm but not bite down. A least he never did on the people he knew.

Ralph was about to call Brian, Kipling's trainer, to come and meet these guys when he heard, "coming through!" from the back of the room. The party parted as a couple of the trainers walked up with Oliver.

Oliver always carried a "Rocky Balboa" look. He was big, tall and quite muscular. At the party, perhaps due to the closeness of the room, he looked bigger and more powerful than ever. Walking upright he headed straight to the leader. The boss of the tribe didn't speak for a while. Oliver had a profound effect on him.

"What the f..k is that?" he finally said.

"He's our bouncer," said one of the trainers, getting a bit upset with these guys intruding on the party. The trainer stopped Oliver. He had positioned him so his face was about three inches from the leader's. Oliver stood staring at the leader without a flinch.

Seeing Oliver from afar could be a bit traumatic but close up was just plain scary. Ralph noticed the tough guy was nervous.

"Yeah, well. Well, look, we know your animals are tame and don't hurt anybody."

With this, Oliver, with his friendly nature, lifted his arm and with a thud, came down hard on the guy's shoulder. This was unplanned for. He just did it on his own. He wasn't being aggressive, just friendly. However, the guy thought differently.

"What's he doing?" asked the leader, starting to panic.

"He's asking you to leave nicely," said the trainer, taking advantage of the unannounced movement. With this, Brian had arrived with Kipling.

"Kipling doesn't want you here either."

Ralph gave Brian a signal to have Kipling do his thing and so he did. Maybe he was in a party mood because the next moment he did an MGM snarl and jumped on the leader. Even Ralph was concerned that this guy was unknown to Kip, and, perhaps Kip would carry his attack too far. Standing, he hovered way above the tribe leader. He was a big tiger and loved to do his snarl. His ears went back, lips pulled up showing huge fangs, and let out a snarl that shook the room. His snarl was scary. It filled the room to such an extent that even the party people backed off a bit.

That did it. The tribe backed out of the restaurant, colliding with Modoc, who was busy eating cake, and took off into the bush. All was quiet until someone spoke up.

"Whew! Those guys need some affection training!"

That broke the ice. Everyone started to laugh. The scare was over but they all agreed they were quite happy they had brought the animals to the party.

Chapter 18

"O.k., everybody, that's a wrap! Six a.m. call at the lake Monday morning."

The crew had just finished shooting a scene with Judy and Clarence. It was Friday evening and everybody was anxious to get home and enjoy the weekend.

Ralph, Ivan, plus a few others were in a huddle talking about the series. Then Jack, the assistant director got on the loudspeaker.

"Hold on, everybody. Mr. Tors has something to say."

The crew always worried when Tors or any of the top people wanted to say a few words. It could be anything from 'thanks for all the hard work,' a major script change, new location or the dreaded words 'the show has been canceled.'

Tors had a slight Hungarian accent and spoke slowly. "Dear friends," he said. "For three years we have worked hard to produce a classic television series - one that has instilled conservation and the love of animals in the hearts of every person who has watched the show. But now, all things must come to an end. And so, I have to inform all of you that Daktari has been canceled."

It was like a hammer slamming down. Many in the crew knew one day it would happen but it hit harder than they ever anticipated. What? Why? Daktari was a top-rated show and getting stronger each week.

"It's all about money," said Tors. "The studios can be most difficult. Sorry. So sorry. We will inform you of the proceedings next week." Then his voice raised a notch. "Meanwhile, we have another show to do so let's make it the best of them all!"

He had tried to be up with that last bit but his emotions failed him, his voice faltered. He could say no more. He walked off; head down, disheartened that the show they had worked so hard for was now coming to an end.

The electrician hit the switch on the powerful big brute light that turns day into night. The whole area was plunged into a dark abyss. Only a sliver of the moon lit the way for those without flashlights. The mood was somber, to say the least.

Judy picked up on Ralph's quiet depression. She thumped him a few times on the leg, trying to get his attention but he just moved on heading towards the wardrobe.

The years of working on Daktari, waking early to interpret the written script, changing wardrobe to fit the scene, traveling where the story dictated, learning to work with many types of animals, and above all seeing it through the eyes of a human had not always been easy for Judy. Her life had become a mixture of human and primate existences.

Sometimes she crisscrossed her learning experiences with the humans with her primate abilities so as better to interpret their actions. Moments of indecision were the hardest, trying to cope with the humans' world. However, each day had furthered the understanding that increased Judy's ability to link her primitive side together with the human and get the job done. Ralph and Charlie spoke often of Judy's amazing comprehension of the human race. Ralph told Charlie of their walks in the forest.

"It hasn't been all work, all learning," he told him. "They were times of bliss."

Whenever Judy and Ralph could break away from the set, they found their happiness in the forest by the house. It was their paradise away from the hustle and bustle of civilization.

The ranch house was born in an ethereal forest of lushness. An abundance of thick greenery put forth a kaleidoscope of color. The vivid forest hues from lime greens to the dark melting chocolate color of the decayed falling trees turned it into a primeval experience. The earth, untouched for centuries, was of a rich, dark burgundy that framed the garden of nature. The chilly cold blue of the mountain streams reflected the sky above. Boulders cast from an unknown source dotted the landscape that built the house, fences and walls. Slices from the jungle's flowers and plants were dug and transplanted into the house and gardens.

So many times Ralph and Judy had walked the deer-created paths that took them deep into mystical places. Soft loam of velvet emerald grass pushed back the forest forming glades of field flowers too precious to disturb. Judy loved the forest. Whether due to just being a forest animal or perhaps it was for the same reasons that Ralph felt - to inhale its beauty, to take in its essence. They walked the paths whenever time allowed. These were the times they connected with the ambiance of the forest.

Judy was fascinated by the wisps of silver white dandelions that floated out of the thickets like little fairies holding umbrellas; they came by the hundreds out of the forest, their source unknown. Ralph would blow away their white tutu's revealing their nudity. Judy used her 'poke the stomach say "hi"' routine to let out some air but it was never enough to do the job. Instead, she would race around trying to catch them.

The two friends picked flowers growing around the roots of the giant fig trees, sat by the icy clear streams that came from underground caves, threw pebbles to see the splash, catching frogs and then watching them scoot away. These were the good times, their times. Not many would understand. That's o.k. They did.

With the cancelation of Daktari, Judy's life became a whirlwind of travel, appearances, and growth. Her days in the human world seemed to overtake her primitive instincts. Normally, a chimp growing up in a civilized world could become quite spoiled, looking at things to benefit themselves, showing false affection to get what they want. Things that best suited them. If they didn't get what they wanted some became quite dangerous.

Judy, on the other hand, due to having it all, became more subdued. She had the best of food, clothes, housing, and friendships and instead of becoming spoiled, became content. Her appreciation showed.

But then, she was different. Whether it was her African experience being saved by Steve and Marti from the poachers or perhaps having a life so totally humanized in society, as she grew, her attitude toward people became more human.

It came slowly, barely noticeable. But change she did.

It seemed that once she had experienced all that she felt was essential, those things became no longer important to her. Where chimps in general didn't give their affection without receiving something in return, Judy gave love without receiving anything for it. She was slowly adapting to the ways of humans and doing things that other captive chimps just didn't do.

Learning to love for the sake of love.

Sharing when food was scarce.

Protecting others at her own risk.

Charlie too had changed over the years. After seeing Judy at the ranch and watching her work, his whole life in primate studies had improved. Never had he witnessed a chimp becoming so civilized. She was the most human chimp he had ever seen.

The more Judy traveled, the more she experienced life in society which, in turn, led her to develop more human traits. Ralph and Judy lived in motels, hotels, slept in cars, trains and even airplanes in the economy section. Their itinerary included schools, lecture halls, wild animal conferences, guest appearances, TV, and movie 'acting.' She won two PATSY Awards for her acting, equivalent to the Academy Award. The PATSY Award honored animal performances. The letters are an acronym and stand for Performing Animal Television Star of the Year.

She was invited along with Ralph and his wife, Toni, and daughter, Tana, by the Hollywood Chamber of Commerce to be guest stars in the Hollywood Christmas parade, a world famous parade that featured many Hollywood film stars and celebrities. Hollywood Boulevard was lit up with Christmas trees, banners, and Santa Claus paraphernalia. Each storefront featured Christmas in its own way. Some had live 'Santas,' others covered the windows with artificial snow. Synthetic reindeers and sleighs were silhouetted on rooftops. Loudspeakers boosted cheery holiday songs.

Marching bands from the local high schools and out-of-state universities were represented with pretty girls twirling batons. The mounted police rode their proud steeds prancing and sidestepping in unison. The entire sidewalk was aglow with the hundreds of movie star plaques embedded in the sidewalk all-leading to the world famous Grauman's Chinese Theater where there were handprints and footprints of world famous movie stars signed in cement.

Ralph arranged for everybody to ride Modoc, their favorite elephant. His crew went to work filing and polishing her nails, hosed her down and scrubbed her skin. A fancy headpiece crowned her head encrusted with giant imitations of rubies, diamonds, and emeralds.

Judy sat up front, dressed in her Christmas elf costume, waving to the thousands of people who lined the boulevard. Sometimes she would do her geek face for the TV cameras. Every so often she would do her war dance, whooping and stomping in a small circle on Mo's head.

Mo always did a little dance when Judy did hers. They were good friends and had spent many hours together. Judy had learned to climb up Mo's leg and with Mo's help, reach her back. Sometimes Judy would hang onto Mo's trunk and be elevated up to her neck.

She gave the finger to certain people in the crowd. Why them, we never knew. Thank goodness it wasn't on TV.

One day when least expected, Charlie received a phone call from Ralph.

"You're not going to believe this one, Charlie," he teased, with a smile in his voice.

"What is it?"

"Judy has another television offer. Well, not so much an offer, but a studio has called me asking me for a dog. A robot dog."

"A robot dog?"

"I think Judy can do it."

Charlie wondered if Ralph had spent too much time in the sun. "I hate to tell you this, Ralph, but Judy isn't a dog."

"I know," Ralph said, "but the studio asked if we had a dog that could act like a 'robot' dog. Apparently, it's for a science fiction series called Battlestar Galactica and the script calls for a robot dog. Anyhow, I found out that they've called every dog trainer in town and they all said they couldn't train a dog to act like a robot. You know, stiff and all that."

"Again, Ralph, what has this got to do with Judy?"

"Well, it's a very successful TV series and for next season, they wanted to add something new. They thought having a robot dog on the show would increase the ratings. They realized that to get one to perform like a robot would be most difficult, but worth a try. They had a suit made that is lightweight and could easily be put on a dog. However, to have a dog perform like a robot would be a challenge – and then a thought came to me - why not train Judy to act like a dog? A robot dog."

"Ralph, really? You think she could do that?"

"Yeah, I absolutely think she can."

"Well, you're the professional. If you think she can, then have at it!"

"Fantastic!"

The next few weeks found them working toward getting Judy ready for her interview. It certainly wasn't Daktari, but then again, if Ralph could convince the 'powers that be' he really had a robot-dog, Judy would find herself once more in front of the camera and once again proving her talent. But there was much to do and in a short time as well. Judy had to learn new behaviors to come off as a legitimate futuristic robot-dog. The studio was constructing a suit that looked like a robot dog yet allowed her to move freely. It was up to her to 'act' stiff-legged. Ralph sent them the measurements and hoped that they didn't ask any questions about the unusual size.

Meanwhile, Judy worked each day learning all the small but important behaviors needed to portray a robot. Ralph showed her how to walk on all four legs without bending her knees and elbows.

When the suit arrived, they were happy to see it fit her perfectly. Moving her head and tail was not to be a problem. They would be moved by remote control. Even the eyes were to be remotely controlled.

The robot suit was made of a lightweight metallic looking material. The head in one part, body in two, and the legs in four. Judy stood, looking like a man having a suit fitted to him. A large mirror was brought in for Ralph see her from different angles. It helped in the training program and Judy enjoyed looking at herself. Whether she had the intellect to fully understand all that was happening was doubtful, but she sure seemed to enjoy herself.

Two weeks later Ralph called the studio. "I think we got your 'robot dog'."

The day arrived. Off to the studios they went. Upon arriving, they dressed Judy in her outfit.

"Wow! She looks great," a smiling Ralph said like a father checking out his little girl for her first school play.

"She sure does look the part. Maybe we can find her a robot girlfriend," quipped Charlie, who had come along for moral support. "Good luck, Judy."

They were to meet on a sound stage. The stage was huge and the producer and executives were sitting in the middle under a series of stage lights.

"Well, my friend," said Mr. Steven, "what have you brought me?"

"I would like to introduce you to the only robot dog in existence," said Ralph, his voice echoing in the huge sound stage. "Go to the men, Judy, go on."

Across the stage came a robot dog, walking stiff-legged. It got to the men, and on Ralph's voice saying "Sit," she sat.

"Well, well, you did it. It's amazing."

"Can we see the dog underneath the costume?" asked the producer.

"Sure."

He walked over and undid the small cord holding the headpiece on. When they saw the chimp face, they nearly fell over.

"Good Lord - a chimp!"

"They're much more practical," Ralph explained. "They're smarter, can make moves dogs can't and realistically, there's really no way a dog could do the same work. Your 'robot-dog' has to take a can off the shelf, climb up on the kitchen sink, hold a glass of water, many, many things dogs can't do – so, voila, a chimp."

181

Judy was a hit. The studio made her a fantastic outfit. It looked like shining gold yet was as light as cotton. When she performed with an off-stage man operating the remote that could wiggle her ears, move her eyes, cock her head and open and close her mouth, she looked as though she had come straight out of the future.

She went on to do the series and was treated as star material. As usual, Judy enjoyed studio work. She loved people fussing over her. Combing her hair, wearing the robot outfit, great food and off stage a small trailer to sleep in if she got tired. Some of the time, Ralph let Charlie bring C.J. along. They were lifelong buddies and she was the happiest when he was on stage watching her perform.

Ralph stayed with her throughout the series, teaching her new behaviors according to the needs of the script. Charlie, with his commitments to the Center, came when he could.

Since Judy's stardom in the galactic series, her IQ seemed to take a jump into a new form of attitude. She moved quicker, seemed to know what to do as it was spoken, learned her behaviors, and was enjoying her upgraded lifestyle.

Ralph and Charlie both agreed to continue working together if more studios jobs happened. As Charlie watched Judy from afar with yet another success, he thought of Marti and Steve and how Judy's life had been an almost rags-to-riches story. He mused about how the people she encountered had supported her throughout - from healing her life-threatening injuries as a very young chimp to believing in her abilities, allowing her to become one of Hollywood's most beloved stars. He was disappointed that the Mathers hadn't been part of her success and he suddenly decided to make an effort to find them. He started by calling Karimi at the plantation.

He knew the communication would be difficult what with the plantation being in the middle of the jungle but he wanted to try it. It took three tries before:

"Karimi, is that you?"

"Yes."

"Can you hear me?"

"Barely, but o.k."

"I wanted to see if you and the plantation are o.k."

"Yes, we are o.k. All is well."

"Are you still having trouble with poachers?"

"Oh, yes! They come back – many times. A dozen, maybe more. They come to fight, Mr. Charlie, they burned some buildings, and hurt a few people, including the neighbors and we fought them, Mr. Charlie. Two die. Yes, two. The police were forced to arrest them. It was too big for them to not prison them. I thought Mr. Steve had told you."

"Mr. Steve? Are they back?"

"Yes, they returned last month. He is next to me now, with a smile on his face."

Charlie could hardly contain his happiness. "Well, for heaven's sake, man, put him on the phone!"

A moment later he heard a voice he hadn't heard in years, and yet it was as if it was yesterday when he was driven to the house by mistake.

"Charlie? Charlie, old man!"

"Steve, you old dog! Why haven't you called?"

"They cut all the lines."

"Who did?"

"Poachers. We got them fixed just now. The neighbors helped. We're still pretty isolated out here, you know. But the neighbors are as sick of them as I am and wanted to finally do these bad people in. A few escaped and the neighbors followed them into the bush."

"What happened?"

"They won't tell me but there are no more bad men. We're happy people."

Charlie knew there were ways of the traditional local tribes that were not revealed to the outside civilized world. Best not to know.

"How's Marti?" Charlie asked, changing the subject.

"She's so much better. Leaving here was the best thing in the world for her. She's happy and well on her way to being one of the best horticulturists around. You should see her flowers; they're the envy of everyone around."

"That's wonderful, Steve."

"She's in town buying new seeds and groceries. She will be so disappointed she missed your call, but now that the lines are back up, we will keep in touch."

"You'd better," said Charlie.

"We got all your letters when we got back. So, our little Judy has made quite a name for herself."

"She certainly has."

"Marti's so proud."

"She should be, Steve, and you too. You're the ones who started her career by taking her in. And Marti should be exceptionally happy with all she did as well. And C.J. is doing well at the Center but Judy lives with Ralph Helfer now, at his ranch. I wrote to you about him in my letters."

"I remember. Good man."

And so they talked for a while longer until their catching up ended with more promises to keep in touch and potential visits to each other in Africa and America. However, by the time Steve and Marti made their visit to see Charlie, Judy, and C.J., it wasn't for the happy occasion they anticipated.

Chapter 19

The years go by much quicker for primates. They shouldn't but they do. They live a life far closer to nature than humans. They benefit from its freshness and its abundance. Judy's life had exceeded her desires. She had lived part primate and part human. Does that not qualify her for a longer existence?

It was in the month of the first falling of the autumn leaves when she fell ill. Never before had she succumbed to an illness. She had always fought herself to the surface to breathe a new breath, to fill her soul with an energy that brought about a new life. Not now. Dr. Andrews had come and gone many times.

"She's failing, Ralph," he said gently. "It's just age. Some primates, just like people, live long lives, other don't."

The best Ralph could figure she was in her 25th year when she took ill.

"Nothing shows," Dr. Andrews said. "All her tests were negative. We took blood, urine, a whole series of test were given."

When it was time to give her a needle, it was easily done. Her experience had been most rewarding. She helped the vet fill the syringe with the medicine, and then helped to poke the needle into her flesh in the proper place and push the syringe to empty the drug into her body in hopes of killing off whatever was causing the problem.

Judy lay in Ralph's bed. Covers pulled up to her chin. Head resting on his pillow. So human.

Ralph was with her as was Charlie. Steve and Marti flew in. Marti, now a grey haired lady, still retained the beauty of her youth and was having a hard time trying to contain herself and needed support to stand.

They spoke briefly to Charlie who introduced them to Ralph. Marti, trying to keep herself from shaking, pushed away anyone trying to help her as she walked into the room and over to the bed.

Judy was sleeping. Her eyes closed. She wore an oxygen mask to help her breathe. As Marti grasped her hand, she woke and seeing Marti, her eyes widened. A small 'woo' came from her in remembrance. She tried to raise her arm to hug the one person in her life she had learned to love first. Marti helped her and the two embraced, holding each other tightly, reliving memories of long ago.

Marti, her face awash with tears, sat with her, asked if she had been a good girl, did she wear her coat when the weather turned cold, did she take her vitamins each day. Judy, her face gaunt, eyes tired, looked longingly at her. Her fingers entwined in hers. Marti spent the time talking to her as though she were a human. Judy listened to every word.

Steve joined them, their hands met in a warm remembrance. Steve helped Marti stand to leave. As they approached the door, they heard Judy in a soft, slurred, weak voice say, "hi, food," but it was there. Marti broke down completely. Steve and Ralph had to help her from the room.

The staff at the ranch, and even some of the original Daktari crew, now working on other shows, one by one, came to say their farewell. Too weak to shake hands, her eyes followed their every move. Every so often, her face would tense up from a pain as it shot through her body. It was as a calling saying it's time to go. Then it would pass, her mouth relaxed, her shoulder settled and her eyes, though sad, returned to their normal clarity.

When Prince, Ralph's German shepherd, came into the room, Judy would stretch out her arm and purse her lips to emit a slight 'ours!' It was her call to him. He would come to the bed and rest his head against her so she could touch him. He licked her hand as he always did. Animals, each in their own way, give each other energy. They gladly transfer it in hopes of healing their friend. A hoarse cough would cause her to reach for a tissue. A taught human trait.

C.J. had come in the early morning, brought there by one of the trainers. He climbed on the bed sitting quietly next to her.

How many times had she and C.J. romped and played, bouncing and giggling on this same bed on their way to sleep. When he was asked to leave, he wrapped his huge hand around the bed frame and refused to go. He sat and preened her, using his long fingers as a comb, occasionally stopping to pick at a bump or ingrown hair. Primates did these things, especially when their mates were sick. They followed them to the edge of the 'crossover' to be sure they were safe, to prepare them for their resting place, to offer their contentment, to shine the sun so their house was never cold.

Judy looked up at Ralph with whom she had spent most of her life. She touched his face with the back of her hand. No need for more. To see, to touch, to know, to love. What more could there possibly be?

Do animals know death? If so, they handle it better than most humans. Do they see the gates, the velvet linings of the hereafter? Perhaps.

It's time to go. Dear Judy. Let it happen. Close your eyes so the warmth of your new birth into another place can blanket you and keep you warm on your travels. The journey is a pleasant one. The crossover is your reward of life.

Ralph's tears fell. Judy watched them with half-closed eyes. She touched where they had landed. She tried so hard to make her geek face to show him all was good. How silly, how wonderful.

Ralph picked her up and held her to him. They felt each other's heartbeat. One beat following the other until they joined and beat in unison.

One beat, two hearts.

Together.

Then suddenly, one was gone. There was one. The silence of the missing one was truly deafening.

Ralph buried Judy on his ranch in their sacred forest alongside others that were once kings and queens during their existence. Modoc, Zamba, Seraing. So many; too many.

One day, I will follow, thought Ralph, and together we will grace the many tomorrows with our gathered love for life.

Epilogue

Living in Africa, touching the cradle of civilization, I see the primal, the primitive, and the spiritual woven together in the great fabric of Life. There is a sense of creation here that I have found nowhere else in my world travels. There is a silent knowing, a deep connection to the earth and all life on it.

I know that every animal has a soul and a right to share this planet with us.

I know they enrich our lives in more ways than we can comprehend, and I know we need to learn to respect their offerings with humility and honor.

Not every animal was, or is, as talented as Judy. She became an ambassador of sorts, showing us how it is possible to co-exist between worlds. She touched everyone, either through her work or simply her friendship - and there is no better life than that.

Judy kissing Ralph